Wild Flowers of Rhodesia

A guide to some of the common wild flowers
of Rhodesia

D. C. H. Plowes
and
R. B. Drummond

Longman Rhodesia

Acknowledgements

Longman Rhodesia (Pvt) Ltd
Beatrice Road, Southerton, Salisbury

*Associated companies, branches and
representatives throughout the world*

© Longman Rhodesia (Pvt) Ltd 1976

First published 1976

ISBN 0 582 64123 3

Printed in Rhodesia by Mardon Printers (Pvt) Limited, Salisbury

We are very grateful to the following people for their assistance:
 Dr L. E. W. Codd, Mrs A. A. Mauve and Dr I. C. Verdoorn of
the Botanical Research Institute, Pretoria, who determined trans-
parencies and specimens of Liliaceae, Iridaceae and Amaryllidaceae;
Rosemary Grosvenor of the National Herbarium, Salisbury, who
helped with the Orchidaceae and the glossary; and Esme Gascoigne
and Pamela Kelly who typed the manuscript.

PUBLISHER'S NOTE
The text of this book was written jointly by R. B. Drummond and
D. C. H. Plowes; the photographs were provided by D. C. H.
Plowes.

Introduction

The aim of this book is to provide a ready means of identifying some of the more showy indigenous flowers that occur in Rhodesia. Although a few of the more attractive rare plants have been included, most of the one hundred and fifty species selected are those which are most commonly found in Rhodesia. In general trees and shrubs have been omitted as the more common of these have already been included in a number of South African and Rhodesian books. Succulents have also been excluded since aloes have been dealt with exhaustively in both Rhodesia and South Africa, and the other succulents form a group that might conveniently be the subject of a future publication.

There are over five thousand species of flowering plants and ferns occurring, wild or naturalised, in Rhodesia, and therefore only a small percentage of the total is included in this book. However, over half the total Rhodesian species of plants consist of ferns, shrubs, trees, grasses and sedges, and a very large number of the others have relatively insignificant flowers or are comparatively rare or restricted in their distribution, so that it would seem probable that no more than three or four hundred species in Rhodesia would be sufficiently common or striking to be of interest to the layman.

Descriptions of the plants featured in this book have been reduced to a minimum, as the accompanying photographs are designed to be the main means of identification. A brief description or reference is given, where relevant, to similar or related species. Information on the Rhodesian flowering period is included, but it is intended only as a very rough guide since the actual duration of flowering is often short and flowering times may vary according to climatic factors.

The distribution of each species, both within Rhodesia and throughout the world, is provided. This information should be especially useful to readers elsewhere in Africa, as most of the plants featured have quite a wide distribution.

Classification and plant names

The only universally meaningful names for plants, and indeed animals, are the scientific names. The International Rules of Botanical Nomenclature govern the application of plant names and therefore eliminate any possibility of confusion.

Common or vernacular names, however, are not bound by any rules and, while many are well known and exact in their application, many are not. The same plant may be known by two or more different names, or alternatively the same name may be used for two different plants. Common names vary also according to local language, this being particularly the case in Rhodesia where there are numerous different African dialects.

Vernacular names exist for about one thousand Rhodesian plants, most of them those which have been used for medicinal or other purposes by the various local African tribes. In European countries also, it was at first only the useful plants that had names. With the advent of printing further names were invented by the herbalists, and others were devised for the published floras of the nineteenth century, so that by the end of the nineteenth century nearly all British plants had common names. Recently it has become the fashion to try to standardise common names both in botany and zoology in Europe and Africa, but difficulties are encountered if too

Plate 1 Limpopo valley, lowveld; *Acacia tortilis* subsp. *heteracantha* and baobabs

Plate 2 Highveld grassland in winter, north of Rusape

Plate 3 Open grassland on highveld, near Headlands

Plate 4 Great Dyke, Mtoroshanga, north-west of Salisbury

wide a geographical area is taken and if the ideal, one name per language, is attempted.

Many people prefer to use a common rather than a scientific name. For this reason all the plants featured in this book have been provided with an English name. In some cases these have had to be specially coined, but where possible, suitable existing names have been used. No attempt has been made to give the vernacular names for the plants featured, as there are often numerous alternatives for each species, and a comprehensive dictionary of vernacular plant names has already been published.

Occasionally the scientific names of plant species have to be altered. These changes, while they may be regrettable and irritating, will result in stability in the long term. A species with a wide range may have been given one name in tropical Africa and a different name in South Africa. When subsequent research shows that both are indeed the same species, the oldest valid name is accepted as being the correct one for the plant, and the other name becomes a synonym. Where applicable, recent synonyms have been given in this book if they have been in general use over the last few years.

The classification of families and genera used in this book follows that of Engler and Prantl. Plants show definite relationships with each other enabling them to be grouped together in categories or taxa of descending order, such as family, genus, species and sub-species. The name of a species is made up of two parts: the name of the genus to which the plant belongs, for example *Gladiolus*, followed by the specific epithet, the name of the actual species, such as *natalensis*. For completeness and accuracy, the name of the author (or usually an abbreviation thereof) is written after the specific name so that, for example, the full designation of the parrot-beak gladiolus is *Gladiolus natalensis* (Eckl.) Reinw. ex Hook.f. In this instance, Ecklon was the first person to describe the plant, and he placed it in the genus *Watsonia* when he published his description; Hooker later transferred the species to the genus *Gladiolus*, but credited Reinwardt

as first suggesting the transfer. In such cases the name of the first author is cited in brackets. However, it is also permissible, and indeed fashionable, to quote only the author who made the actual transfer.

As is the case with most species, *Gladiolus natalensis* consists of many individuals in populations scattered throughout many countries, all distinguished slightly from one another by characters such as flower colour, stature and leaf width. However, all these individual gladioli are so similar in appearance and structure that they are best regarded as one species. Furthermore, *G. natalensis* is so similar in many characters to *G. melleri* and all other species of *Gladiolus* that one has no hesitation in placing them all in the same genus. Similarly, *Gladiolus*, *Dierama*, *Anomatheca* and *Lapeirousia* resemble each other in certain important characteristics and are therefore placed together in the same family, the Iridaceae.

Within a species there may be further subdivisions or groupings, and these, in descending order, are subspecies (subsp.), variety (var.) and form (f.). The term subspecies is used to distinguish populations which differ somewhat from the type but are not sufficiently different to be regarded as a separate species. A subspecies normally occupies a distinct geographical area, quite separate either spatially or eco-logically from that occupied by related subspecies. The term variety is reserved for a taxon which occurs sufficiently frequently so as not to be a freak or chance mutation, but does not occur as a pure population in a clearly defined area. The term form is rarely used.

Collecting and identification

There is still much to be learnt about almost all of our wild plants. In what parts of Rhodesia do they occur? At what altitudes and in what situations are they to be found? In what type of soil do they grow? What is the parent rock from which the soil is derived? What are the dominant trees or other plants with which they are associated? When do they flower, and what are the seeds or fruits like? To what uses are they put? Are they locally endangered? How can they best

Plate 5 Msasa *(Brachystegia spiciformis)* woodland in spring, Umtali

Plate 6 Victoria Falls; Kalahari Sand overlying basalt

Plate 7 Matopo hills south of Bulawayo

Plate 8 Matabeleland; acacia veld north of Bulawayo

be propagated? What are the local African names? Anyone who collects specimens and records this kind of information will therefore be making a useful contribution to scientific knowledge.

Specimens, either the entire plant (folded once or more often if necessary) or a branch bearing leaves and flowers, or leaves and fruit, can be pressed and dried between several layers of folded newspaper. The papers should be changed several times while the plant is drying in order to prevent mould. The best results are achieved by arranging the plant whilst it is still fresh. Bulky flower heads are most successfully dealt with by being sliced in half longitudinally, as they then dry out more quickly and uniformly and there is less danger of the flowers being shed. Immersion in petrol or hot water is useful as it kills the tissues and thus prevents flowers or leaves from dropping; it is a particularly suitable method of dealing with some of the succulent species such as aloes, red-hot pokers and erythrinas (kaffir-boom). Delicate flowers, such as those of the morning-glory family, should be placed between extra pieces of tissue paper and not moved until fully dry. A plant press can be made by stapling together strips of plywood to form a lattice, which is then nailed to a square frame. The specimen, in its papers, is placed between two frames which are tied or strapped together. Alternatively, the papers can be placed between sheets of cardboard and weighted down with bricks or books.

Pressed and dried specimens, preferably two for each plant, should be forwarded to The National Herbarium, P.O. Box 8100, Causeway. These can be sent post free if marked 'O.G.S. — Specimens for Identification'. Once the determinations have been completed, the collector will be informed of the name of each specimen.

The collector should retain a sample of each plant for his own reference. Notes on each specimen, numbered consecutively, should be recorded in duplicate so that a copy can accompany each species sent to the herbarium. These notes should give the name of the collector, the date of collection, the locality, details of habitat and distribution, and such information as is not discernible from the dried specimen, for example flower colour, height of plant, and type of root or bulb.

Rhodesian habitats

The species notes include a brief mention of the type of Rhodesian habitat in which the plant is normally found. Elsewhere conditions may be different, and the same species may be encountered at higher or lower altitudes as one proceeds further north or south respectively.

The South African terms highveld, middleveld and lowveld have been used to indicate the main altitudinal zones. The lowveld is the hot dry area lying below 800 m. The rainfall is usually under 400 mm a year, the evaporation rate is high and frosts are very infrequent. Two trees characteristic of this area are the baobab (*Adansonia digitata*) and mopane (*Colophospermum mopane*). The latter grows principally on the more alkaline soils where there is impeded drainage. Other common trees are species of *Acacia*, *Combretum*, *Commiphora* and *Grewia* (Plate 1). Most of the lowveld is dry deciduous woodland in which, due to over-grazing, perennial grasses are often replaced by annuals. There is little open grassland except on some of the heavy black clays overlying basalt. The lowveld occupies the valleys of the Limpopo, Sabi and Zambezi river systems.

The highveld forms the watershed areas and lies along two axes; one runs from Bulawayo to Salisbury and beyond to Umvukwes, with spurs branching north-west to Karoi and south-east to Fort Victoria; the other runs from Inyanga via Rusape and Marandellas to Salisbury (Plates 2 and 3). The Great Dyke, five hundred kilometres in length, follows the north-south watershed. It has a high proportion of serpentine and chrome-bearing rocks and thus provides a specialised habitat that has given rise to several endemic species (Plate 4).

The highveld receives a good summer rainfall, although this decreases in Matabeleland south of Gwelo. Frosts are frequent from

Plate 9 Mount Inyangani and Matenderere river, Inyanga

Plate 10 Chimanimani mountains, Melsetter

June to August, but the climate is moderate at most times of the year. Most of this watershed country lies between 1 200 and 1 600 m. Much of the highveld is open grassland or open deciduous woodland with either msasa (*Brachystegia spiciformis*) or mfuti (*B. boehmii*) being the dominant tree. These, together with the mountain acacia (*B. glaucescens*), provide a spectacular sight in spring (Plate 5).

Between the highveld and the lowveld is the middleveld. Rainfall is lower and droughts are more frequent here than on the watershed areas. Msasa is largely replaced by mnondo (*Julbernardia globiflora*) on the granite sands in the eastern half of the country, but large areas between Bulawayo and the Victoria Falls are covered with deep Kalahari Sand overlying sandstone or basalt. This was originally wind-borne, but is now stabilised and carries a luxuriant woodland in which the rhodesian teak (*Baikiaea plurijuga*) is a prominent species (Plate 6).

Granite is the type of rock found over about two-thirds of Rho-

desia. It normally gives rise to a coarse-grained sand of low fertility and is also responsible for one of the most characteristic of Rhodesian landscapes: rocky kopjes rising above the surrounding bush. One of the most extensive concentrations of these kopjes is to be found in the Matopo hills south of Bulawayo (Plate 7). On the drier granite sands, mnondo gives way to mangwe (*Terminalia sericea*). On the reddish brown loams of Matabeleland which overlie schist and basic rocks such as dolerite and andesite, various thorn trees (*Acacia* spp.) are the principal woodland constituents (Plate 8).

The spine of high ground which forms the international boundary between Mozambique and Rhodesia constitutes a further altitudinal zone. It stretches from Inyanga in the north to Chipinga in the south, and includes Mount Inyangani, which is 2 550 m in height, and the Chimanimani mountains at Melsetter, which reach 2 400 m (Plates 9 and 10). Both mountain masses, apart from being extremely attractive scenically, are very interesting botanically as they support a number of endemic species and form the meeting point for the flora of the temperate southern mountains and that of the more tropical African mountain ranges.

Along the eastern border, particularly in the Pungwe, Honde, Burma and Rusitu valleys and around Mount Selinda, the higher rainfall causes lush conditions, and relic patches of climax evergreen forest still remain in protected sites. On the eastern slopes of Mount Inyangani near the tea estates of the Pungwe valley, rainfall in excess of 5 000 mm a year has been recorded, although half of that figure is more usual, and here bamboo (*Oxytenanthera abyssinica*) is a major constituent of the pioneer forest vegetation. These climatic conditions enable this area to support a flora which is very distinctive.

Conservation and protection

A bold approach has been adopted with the introduction of the new Parks and Wild Life Act of 1975 in that the conservation of flora and fauna on private land (apart from specially protected species) now becomes the responsibility of the landowner and local conservation committees. Furthermore, all legislation relating to the protection of flora has been consolidated into one Act, thus making it more easy to understand and administer.

The more sought-after species are afforded extra protection by being listed in a special schedule. However, provision is made for the issue of permits to collect these plants for scientific or other purposes. Permission to collect other species lies with the owner of the land or, in the case of public land, a designated official.

The collecting and selling of flame-lilies, sabi stars, various aloes and cycads, as well as certain orchids and other plants, is now controlled. It is hoped that in future these plants will be supplied to gardeners by registered nurserymen. When it is permissible to collect wild plants for growing in gardens, damage to the beauty of the veld can be minimised by taking cuttings, root divisions, or small seedlings only. Furthermore, such collecting should be confined to areas not normally accessible or visible to others. From time to time plant rescue operations, such as occur when an area is to be inundated by a dam, provide opportunities for plant lovers to add to their collections and ensure a safe home for specimens which would otherwise have been destroyed.

It is hoped that this book, by acquainting the general public with this country's floral wealth, will lead to a determined effort by all to preserve for posterity the flowers and the countryside which contribute so much to Rhodesia's unique charm.

Plate 11   Plate 12

1 Zantedeschia albomaculata (Hook.) Baill.

Plate 11

subsp. **albomaculata**

spotted-leaved arum-lily

Family Araceae

Synonyms *Z. oculata; Z. tropicalis*

Flowers December to January.

Habitat Damp ground, marshy areas by streams, at the base of ant-heaps in vleis, amongst bracken and in grassland on hills.

Distribution From Salisbury eastwards to Inyanga and then southwards where it is found in the mist belt in hilly areas as far south as Mount Selinda. It extends northwards into Zambia and Malawi, westwards into Angola and southwards through the eastern Transvaal to Natal and the eastern Cape.

General *Z. albomaculata* loses its leaves and dies down in the dry season. Despite the specific name which means 'white spotted', the leaves vary even in a single population from conspicuously spotted to completely unspotted. The spathe colour may vary from white or cream to pale yellow or pink. Most populations in Rhodesia consist of plants which have pale yellow spathes with a maroon blotch at the base. Enclosed in the spathe is the spadix which bears male flowers above and female flowers below.

Two other subspecies of *Z. albomaculata* occur in South Africa. The genus contains five other species all confined to South Africa; the best known of these is *Z. aethiopica*, the white arum-lily, which has been in cultivation since the seventeenth century.

Arum-lilies are sometimes still referred to as callas or richardias. *Calla* however is a distinct South American genus, and *Richardia* is a South American genus of Rubiaceae, widely naturalised in Africa. The genus was named in honour of Giovanni Zantedeschi (1773-1846), an Italian botanist and physician.

2 Commelina erecta L.

Plate 12

subsp. **livingstonii** (C.B.Cl.) J. K. Morton

woodland blue commelina

Family Commelinaceae

Flowers November to April.

Habitat Occurring at all but the highest altitudes, most commonly in woodland and amongst rocks in full sun or partial shade.

Distribution Subspecies *livingstonii* is widespread in Africa, extending from Senegal to the Cape. Subspecies *erecta* is fairly common in Africa, but occurs also in America, Asia and Australia.

General *Commelina* is readily distinguished from other genera of the same family: it has a characteristic folded spathe which protects the flower buds and fruits, and from which flowers are produced in succession, only one or two being visible at a time.

The delicate flowers last only a few hours. In *C. erecta*, as in most species of *Commelina*, each flower has three inconspicuous sepals, and one inconspicuous and two showy petals. There are three fertile stamens and three smaller cross-shaped staminodes; the filaments of both the stamens and staminodes, like the showy petals, are blue.

The genus contains more than two hundred and thirty species of which some twenty occur in Rhodesia. The best known species are *C. benghalensis*, a common garden and agricultural weed which, besides having the normal blue flowers, produces self-fertilising white underground flowers, and *C. africana*, a very common and variable yellow-flowered species.

Linnaeus, in an allusion to the two showy petals and the inconspicuous one, named the genus after the three members of the Commelin family who lived in the eighteenth and nineteenth centuries — brothers Johann and Caspar Commelin were well known botanists, while the third brother died before accomplishing anything in botany.

Plate 13   Plate 14

Plate 15   Plate 16

3 Gloriosa superba L. *Plates* 13, 14 and 15

flame-lily

Family Liliaceae

Flowers December to February.

Habitat Most frequent in woodland on the highveld, but also among bracken along forest margins at higher altitudes, and in woodland in the lowveld.

Distribution Throughout tropical Africa and extending as far south as the eastern Cape. It occurs also in tropical India, Sri Lanka and the Malagasy Republic.

General *G. superba* is an extremely variable species. The flower colour ranges from pure yellow through to red with many combinations of these colours. The form of the petals varies from fairly narrow with wavy margins to wider with less wavy margins. The habit varies from erect with leaves without or almost without tendrils, to climbing with long slender tendrils at the tips of the leaves. The extreme forms have been regarded as distinct species, but it seems best to consider the genus as having only one wide ranging variable species. *G. virescens* and *G. simplex* are names which have been widely used in southern Africa but which fall into synonymy under *G. superba*.

This species has in recent years come to be regarded as Rhodesia's national flower. In the past its numbers have been somewhat reduced in the neighbourhood of the main population centres by the activities of flower sellers and gardeners. It is now one of the specially protected indigenous plants scheduled under the Parks and Wild Life Act.

All parts of the plant are toxic to both human beings and stock, although stock poisoning is rare since the plant is evidently not palatable and is usually avoided. The powdered tuber is employed in African medicine to relieve toothache and other ailments, but its use is dangerous and sometimes causes death.

4 Eucomis autumnalis (Mill.) Chittenden *Plate* 16

pineapple flower

Family Liliaceae

Synonym *E. undulata*

Flowers December to March.

Habitat Woodland and grassland at vlei margins, on damp rocky ground, in Rhodesia from 1 200 to 2 000 m.

Distribution From Inyanga to Buhera and scattered along the central watershed to Gwelo and Bulalima-Mangwe. It occurs from Zambia and Malawi south to the eastern Cape.

General There are several species of *Eucomis*, all of which are confined to southern Africa. *E. autumnalis* is the most widespread and the only one to occur in Rhodesia. Its whitish to green flowers, which have no purple colouring, and its unspotted leaves separate it from some of its relatives.

The characteristic green leaf-like bracts at the top of the inflorescence serve to distinguish *Eucomis* from other genera of bulbous Liliaceae and also give rise to its common name. The generic name *Eucomis*, which means 'beautiful hair', is an allusion to these bracts. The specific name is not particularly apt in Rhodesia as the plant tends to flower at the height of the rains, in summer in fact and not in autumn.

The bulb is widely used by folk practitioners in South Africa to treat a variety of unrelated ailments, from abdominal disorders in human beings to gallsickness in cattle. There is, however, some evidence to suggest that the bulbs are toxic, although they have not been positively incriminated as poisonous to livestock in Rhodesia.

Plate 17

Plate 18

Plate 19

5 Kniphofia linearifolia Bak.   *Plates* 17 and 18

common red-hot poker

Family Liliaceae

Synonyms *K. longiflora; K. rhodesiana*

Flowers February to April.

Habitat Vleis and damp hillsides in bracken and rank grass.

Distribution Along the watershed from Salisbury to Umtali, being especially common near Marandellas and in the higher areas of eastern Rhodesia adjoining Mozambique. It extends northwards into Malawi and Zambia and southwards through the eastern Transvaal to the eastern Cape.

General *K. linearifolia* makes a spectacular sight in many of the Mashonaland vleis, often occurring in dense stands with flower stems reaching 1,5 m in height. The stamens of this species are only just exserted during flowering and the raceme of flowers is no more than 12 cm long. It is the most widespread red-hot poker in Rhodesia and South Africa. *K. splendida*, the only other species found in Rhodesia, occurs sparingly in the Inyanga and Melsetter districts. It tends to be more robust, having a longer raceme of flowers (up to 20 cm or more), and stamens well exserted during and after flowering.

A genus consisting of sixty-five species, *Kniphofia* is confined to Africa except for one species recorded from the Yemen and two from the Malagasy Republic. There are forty-five species to be found in South Africa, only two of which extend into tropical Africa. None of the other twenty tropical species reaches as far south as Rhodesia.

Most of the cultivated red-hot pokers are derived from the Cape *K. uvaria*, or from *K. linearifolia* or allied species. The generic name honours J. H. Kniphof (1704-1763), a Professor of medicine at Erfurt University in Germany.

6 Ammocharis coranica (Ker-Gawl.) Herb.   *Plate* 19

southern ammocharis

Family Amaryllidaceae

Flowers October to December with the first soaking rains.

Habitat Open areas in *Acacia* or mopane woodland, especially on silty or alluvial soils on flat ground.

Distribution Fairly widely distributed in South Africa, Botswana and South West Africa; it extends into southern Angola and southern and south-western Rhodesia.

General *Ammocharis* is an African genus containing four species, but only the two species included in this book are to be found in Rhodesia or South Africa. Both species usually occur in colonies which make a colourful display when in flower. The strap-like curved leaves lie in two opposite sets; they are usually grazed or die off flush to ground level, and therefore have a square-tipped appearance when emerging the following season. The bulbs are large and have a brown outer covering. These plants are best grown from seed as they do not take kindly to transplanting. They require a warm sunny position and a fertile soil which should not be too acid.

The Swazi people grind the charred bulbs of *A. coranica* into a tar-like paste which they use for making headrings for chiefs and headmen. The same paste is used in the north-eastern Transvaal for water-proofing earthenware.

The generic name is derived from the Greek and means 'sand beauty'. The specific name means 'from the Koranna country', an early name for the northern Cape and Botswana.

Plate 20

Plate 22

Plate 21

Plate 23

7 Ammocharis tinneana (Kotschy & Peyr.) Milne-Redh. *Plate* 20

northern ammocharis

Family Amaryllidaceae

Flowers October to December with the first heavy rains.

Habitat Occurs on a variety of soils, often on rich sandy alluvium. It is most frequent in mopane woodland in association with acacias, baobabs and combretums.

Distribution Widespread at lower altitudes in Rhodesia; particularly abundant in parts of the Zambezi valley, and extending up the tributaries to Que Que and Hartley; found also in the Sabi valley and in the southern lowveld. It has not been recorded in the west of Rhodesia, but one would expect it to occur there. This is a very widespread species, occurring from the Sudan and Ethiopia south to South West Africa and Botswana.

General While similar in many ways to *A. coranica*, this species can be readily distinguished by the more delicate and slender perianth lobes and the shorter flower stalks which are only up to half the length of the tube of the flowers; in *A. coranica* the individual flower stalks are as long as, or longer than, the tube of the flower. It normally grows in small or large colonies which make a spectacular show.

The position of the ovary is one of the characters which separates members of the Amaryllis family from those of the Lily family: the ovary is superior or enclosed by the perianth in the Liliaceae and inferior in the Amaryllidaceae. Another important character distinguishing most members of this family is the arrangement of the flowers in an umbel subtended by at least two large bracts which are sometimes conspicuously coloured.

This species is named after A. Tinné who collected the plant in the Sudan in 1873.

8 Boophone disticha (L.f.) Herb. *Plates* 21, 22 and 23

veld fan; wind ball

Family Amaryllidaceae

Flowers September to November.

Habitat Open grassland and woodland at most altitudes and on a wide variety of soils; it is perhaps most frequent on granite sandveld.

Distribution Widespread in Rhodesia and particularly common in the east and along the central watershed; it extends from Uganda and Kenya to the Cape.

General The flowers, conspicuous after veld fires, grow from a large bulb which often partly emerges above the ground. When flowering it will be seen to be closely related to the common fireball (*Haemanthus multiflorus*). After flowering the stalklets of the flowers increase in length to about 30 cm and become rigid, so that the whole seed head forms a sphere up to 60 cm in diameter. When this becomes detached it is rolled along by the wind, thus scattering the seed. The leaves appear after the flowers and are arranged like an upright fan.

Stock frequently nibble the leaves, apparently without ill effect. The bulbs, however, were used as a source of arrow-poison by the Hottentots and Bushmen, but there seems to be no evidence of their having been used in this way in Rhodesia or East Africa. Toxic alkaloids have been isolated from the bulb. It is fairly widely used medicinally by the Shona, for example, as a dressing for sores and wounds. It is also used to instigate possession during the initiation of African herbalists or witchdoctors. It is best to regard all parts of the plant as toxic.

The name *Boophone* means 'ox-killer'. The specific name refers to the two-ranked leaves which all occur in the same plane.

Plate 24

Plate 25

Plate 26

9 Crinum graminicola Verdoorn   *Plates* 24 and 25

grassland crinum

Family   Amaryllidaceae

Flowers   October to November.

Habitat   Open granite sandveld, in shallow pockets of soil on granite outcrops or on grassland overlying sandstone.

Distribution   Scattered along the central watershed from Salisbury eastwards, and in eastern Rhodesia occurring from 1 100 to 1 600 m above sea level. It is also found in central and northern Transvaal and in adjacent areas of Natal.

General   This magnificent species comes into flower with the first rains. It occurs in several colour forms ranging from white with a deep pink stripe through increasing amounts of pink to a striking carmine red.

The broadly flared flowers have very short stalklets, pale yellow anthers, long-beaked fruits and broad flat leaves with fringed margins, normally without undulations. As in other species of *Crinum*, the leaves die off or are grazed back to the ground level during the dry season; when growth recommences, the previous season's leaves grow out again with truncated tips as if they had been cut off with shears. This species somewhat resembles *C. delagoense*, but the latter differs in having fruit with longer stalklets and without beaks.

The name *Crinum* is derived from the Greek word for lily. The specific name means 'inhabitant of grassland'.

10 Crinum minimum Milne-Redh.   *Plate* 26

dwarf crinum

Family   Amaryllidaceae

Flowers   October to December.

Habitat   It is most frequent at low altitudes on dry sandy alluvial soil in open areas in mopane and other types of woodland.

Distribution   In Rhodesia it is found chiefly in the main river valleys and occurs from Tanzania southward to the Transvaal, Botswana and South West Africa.

General   This species is distinguished from other Rhodesian crinums by the fact that it has only a single flower per inflorescence. When bulbs have produced offsets several plants may often produce flowers close together. All the plants in an area will flower soon after the first soaking rains of the season, but the flowering period is brief. Each bulb may produce several flowers in succession during the first weeks of the rains.

The small bulbs, only 3 to 5 cm in diameter and up to 8 cm long, and the narrow leaves, no wider than 4 mm, readily distinguish *C. minimum* from all other Rhodesian species except *C. baumii*. The latter occurs locally in the Sanyati Tribal Trust Land and has several flowers per inflorescence and a long slender perianth tube up to 12 cm long.

Plate 27   Plate 28

Plate 29

11 Crinum macowanii Bak.   *Plates* 27 and 28

common vlei crinum

Family Amaryllidaceae

Flowers November to December.

Habitat Stream banks and vleis.

Distribution In Rhodesia it is very common in parts of the central watershed and at medium to low altitudes in the east. It occurs from Angola, Zambia, Malawi and Mozambique southwards to the Cape.

General This plant is a familiar sight in the vleis near Marandellas and Salisbury. It can be distinguished from other species by the pendulous bell-shaped flowers which have black anthers. The flower colour is usually white with pink stripes, but it may vary from almost pure white to pink. The flowers possess a powerful scent which develops only in the evening. The fruit retains the style base as a long beak. The wide leaves have wavy margins and arch from the large underground bulbs which may reach 25 cm or more in diameter.

Ten species of *Crinum* have been recorded in Rhodesia. There is still a great deal to be learned about the distribution of these and related species in neighbouring countries. The main reason for the lack of knowledge of this genus is that it is difficult to make satisfactory dried specimens of crinums, as when they are pressed they lose many of the characters they had in life. Over the years this has made comparison of one species with another difficult.

C. macowanii is named after Professor Peter MacOwan (1830-1909), a well known Cape botanist.

12 Crinum paludosum Verdoorn   *Plate* 29

pan crinum

Family Amaryllidaceae

Flowers November to December.

Habitat Seasonably flooded pans at low altitudes, often in mopane woodland.

Distribution So far recorded in Rhodesia only from the Sabi valley, but it may prove to be more widespread; also occurs from South West Africa eastwards through Botswana to parts of the Transvaal and Zululand.

General The pan crinum grows in dense, sometimes very large, colonies in shallow water, forming a most attractive sight when in flower. Apart from its distinctive habitat, the pan crinum may be distinguished from closely related species by its suberect predominantly white flowers which lack the marked pink or red stripe of the perianth lobe characteristic of some of the other species. The fruits are not beaked and the leaves are relatively narrow (up to 5 cm in width) and arching.

The specific name *paludosum* means 'growing in marshy places'.

Crinum is a large genus with over one hundred and fifty described species occurring from the tropics of both the Old and New Worlds and extending into the temperate regions of both hemispheres. Over half this number are described from Africa, but it seems likely that, when the entire genus is adequately monographed, the number of species will decrease. Dr I. C. Verdoorn's excellent account of the twenty-one South African species, published in 1973, has made it possible to classify the Rhodesian species.

Plate 30

Plate 31

Plate 32

13 Haemanthus multiflorus Martyn   *Plates* 30 and 31

common fireball

Family Amaryllidaceae

Flowers October to December.

Habitat It has a very wide ecological range, occurring in low altitude and montane forest, in grassland and woodland, and on termite mounds; in drier areas it is confined to alluvial soils on river banks.

Distribution It occurs in all parts of Rhodesia except in very low rainfall areas, and is widely distributed from Senegal to Arabia and south to South West Africa, Botswana and the Transvaal, with a distinct subspecies extending from Swaziland to the eastern Cape.

General Because of its wide distribution and varying habitat, *H. multiflorus* shows considerable diversity of form. For instance, the number of flowers can range from ten to over two hundred in a single inflorescence, the diameter of which can vary from 5 to 26 cm. Leaf development is affected by moisture conditions so that in forest the leaves will usually appear simultaneously with the flowers, but in woodland in drier areas the leaves will not appear until after the flowers. The false stems of the leaves and the peduncles are often spotted with brownish red dots.

Only one other species of *Haemanthus*, *H. puniceus*, occurs in Rhodesia besides the two included here. It is a rare plant of the Matopos area, and may be distinguished by its large broad bracts which often grow above the flowers. It does not have a continuous distribution, being fairly common from the Transvaal to the eastern Cape and then appearing in south-western Tanzania and Ethiopia.

The generic name means 'blood flower'.

14 Haemanthus pole-evansii Oberm.   *Plate* 32

inyanga fireball

Family Amaryllidaceae

Flowers December to February.

Habitat Montane evergreen forest between 1 500 and 2 000 m.

Distribution Known only from the eastern slopes of Mount Inyangani, the Pungwe gorge and south towards the Mtarazi falls.

General Although related to *H. multiflorus*, this species differs considerably in the length of the perianth tube, the width of the perianth segments and the larger dimensions of the stamens. Indeed, in general appearance it looks more like a deep salmon pink *Agapanthus*, and, at first sight, one might not even regard it as belonging to the genus *Haemanthus*. A forest glade with a group of the one metre tall flowers is an unforgettable sight. Even when the flowers fade the heads are still attractive because, like other species in the genus, the green ovaries develop into a bunch of brilliant scarlet berries. It can be readily grown from seed and, although only recently discovered, is already established and well known throughout the horticultural world.

The plant was in cultivation in Rhodesia as early as 1947, but it was not until Reginald John Pole Evans (son of Dr I. B. Pole Evans, the well known former Chief Botanist of South Africa) drew his father's attention to it, that it was sent to Pretoria and described.

Plate 33   Plate 34

15 Hypoxis obtusa Burch.   *Plate 33*

yellow star

Family Hypoxidaceae

Flowers October to January.

Habitat Grassland and the intermediate zone between vlei and woodland, mainly at altitudes above 1 300 m.

Distribution Common in the eastern highlands and along the central watershed. It extends northwards to Tanzania and is widespread in South Africa, especially in the highveld of the Transvaal and Natal.

General Many species of *Hypoxis* have been described, but the specific limits are in many instances ill defined and it seems certain that, when a revision of the genus is undertaken, a broad view will have to be adopted and the number of species reduced.

The golden yellow star-shaped flowers of this and related species are characteristic of the grasslands of southern Africa. The ovary below the flower develops into the capsule, the top of which comes off like a cap, thus allowing the seeds to be shed. The root-stock is a yellow-fleshed corm covered with fibrous bases of old leaves.

The corms are used medicinally by the Shona to treat abdominal and heart pains, coughs and many other complaints. The leaves of some species are plaited to make ropes.

The name *Hypoxis* means 'sharp below', and it has been suggested that this may refer to the base of the capsule. Another theory is that it may apply to the sharp apices of the lower petals.

16 Xerophyta villosa (Bak.) L. B. Smith & Ayensu   *Plate 34*

hairy fibre-stem

Family Velloziaceae

Flowers November to January.

Habitat In soil pockets on granite outcrops, often with resurrection plant (*Myrothamnus flabellifolius*).

Distribution Throughout the granite areas of Rhodesia, especially in places subject to mist and drizzle. It also occurs in Zambia and the Transvaal.

General Until recently species of *Xerophyta* were included in *Vellozia*, a genus which is now considered to be confined to Panama and South America. There are some twenty-five African species with three others occurring in the Malagasy Republic and one recorded from Arabia. At least seven species are found in Rhodesia, varying from *X. equisetoides*, which may occasionally reach heights of over 2 m, to the dwarf *X. humilis*, which is common in depressions in mopane woodland and never exceeds 3 cm in height.

The larger species share the character of having tough, comparatively slender central stems which are surrounded by the fibrous remains of leaf bases. In the dry season after fires the stems appear stark and black, apparently dead. However, soon after the first rains they spring to life and produce grass-like leaves and mauve-blue flowers. All the plants in the area come into bloom at the same time but the flowers last for only three to four days.

The stems are sometimes cut into blocks and used as pan scourers, or are used as supports on which to grow epiphytic orchids.

The name *Xerophyta* means 'dry plant' and the specific name refers to the hairs on the ovaries and leaves.

Plate 35   Plate 36

17 Babiana hypogea Burch.   *Plate 35*

dwarf babiana

Family Iridaceae

Flowers January to May.

Habitat Open grassland, *Brachystegia* woodland and edges of vleis; found also on leached acidic sandy soils in abandoned cultivations.

Distribution Along the watershed in Rhodesia, extending north to the Zambezi escarpment and into Zambia, across to South West Africa and Botswana, and south to the Transvaal, Natal and the northern Cape.

General This is a handsome member of a genus which is noted for its striking flowers. It grows from a deep seated, fibrous coated corm. The leaves and flowers arise directly from the corm with their 10 to 15 cm long stalks remaining below ground. The above ground portion of the leaf may be up to 30 cm long, but the flowers are produced at ground level in congested inflorescences. The succession of mauve-blue sweetly scented flowers makes it a plant worth cultivating. It does best in full sun on a well drained acid soil.

Some sixty species are known, almost all of which are confined to the Cape.

The corms are eaten raw by local Africans.

The name *Babiana* is thought to be a corruption of the early Cape Dutch word for a baboon and, indeed, baboons and other animals will dig up and eat the corms. The specific name refers to the inflorescence which is underground before the flowers open.

18 Dierama pendulum (L.f.) Bak.   *Plate 36*

common harebell

Family Iridaceae

Flowers September to December.

Habitat Damp grassy stream banks and vleis at high altitudes.

Distribution Mountains on the Rhodesia/Mozambique border, extending northwards to Tanzania and southwards along the Drakensberg mountains to the eastern Cape.

General Harebells are popular garden plants in temperate areas as they have a long flowering period and are easy to grow. The flowers hang by thread-like stalks and tremble in the slightest breeze. The flowering stems may reach 2 m or more in favourable localities.

The genus *Dierama* was revised by N. E. Brown in 1929 and no fewer than twenty-five species were recognised. A few more have been described since then, making a total of about thirty, but many of them are very similar and not easily separable. The genus is in need of revision and it is with some hesitance that much of the Rhodesian material has been assigned to *D. pendulum*. It seems that at least one other species of *Dierama* occurs in Rhodesia in the Inyanga district. This species differs from *D. pendulum* in having more or less erect inflorescences, much narrower leaves and a more delicate habit.

D. pendulum was the earliest species to be described and has been in cultivation since 1781. Fortunately many of its Rhodesian localities are now within the boundaries of the National Parks and therefore the plants are afforded some protection.

The name *Dierama* means 'funnel' and refers to the shape of the flower.

Plate 37   Plate 38

19 Gladiolus gazensis Rendle *Plate 37*

gazaland gladiolus

Family Iridaceae

Flowers September to November or December.

Habitat Short open grassland on hillsides or vlei margins, or among rocks in shallow loams overlying shales and sandstone.

Distribution On the central watershed from Marandellas eastwards and on mountains and hills along the Rhodesia/Mozambique border.

General The branched flowering stems are about 30 to 60 cm tall and are usually produced before the rains. Burning seems to stimulate flowering as it does with many other spring flowers. A related and very handsome species, apparently undescribed, flowers towards the end of the rains and occurs commonly on high ground from Inyanga to Melsetter. A charming little species occurring on the quartzite of the Chimanimanis, and a showy species found in the Haroni/Lusitu valley and in Mozambique may also prove to be new.

The sword-like leaves gave rise to the name *Gladiolus* which was the term given to the short sword used by Roman gladiators. The specific name refers to the area where C. F. M. Swynnerton discovered the species, that is, the outskirts of Chirinda forest at Mount Selinda and Mount Pene near Melsetter. Swynnerton defines Gazaland thus: 'The tract we call Gazaland extends roughly from some distance to the south of Delagoa Bay to the Umvumvumvu, Lusitu and Buzi rivers, the sea bounding on the East and the Sabi river on the West.

20 Gladiolus melleri Bak. *Plate 38*

tropical pink gladiolus

Family Iridaceae

Flowers September to November.

Habitat In grassland in the marginal zone between woodland and vlei.

Distribution All along the central watershed from Umtali to the Matopo hills, and also in the Lake Kyle area. It extends northwards through tropical Africa to northern Nigeria.

General The flowers are noticeable when the grass begins to flush green after the veld has been burnt. The flowering stems are about 40 to 50 cm tall and appear before the leaves. The bright splashes of colour made by the deep salmon pink flowers enliven the wayside for motorists travelling between Umtali and Salisbury in early spring. As with most early flowering species, the capsules ripen and shed the seeds within a few weeks. This attractive species makes a fine show in the garden; it grows readily and multiplies rapidly in cultivation if given a rich well watered soil and a sunny position.

The genus *Gladiolus* has about one hundred and eighty species of which over a hundred occur south of the Limpopo. About nine species occur in Rhodesia. Apart from *G. natalensis* and *G. unguiculatus*, *G. melleri* has the most extensive range of all gladioli and is also one of the most distinctive. It was named after Dr C. J. Meller who accompanied Dr Livingstone from 1860 to 1863 and made the first collection of *G. melleri* by the Zambezi in Mozambique.

Plate 39

Plate 40

Plate 41

21 Gladiolus natalensis (Eckl.) Reinw. ex Hook.f. *Plates* 39 and 40

parrot-beak gladiolus; natal gladiolus

Family Iridaceae

Synonyms *G. psittacinus; G. primulinus; G. quartinianus*

Flowers December to May.

Habitat Open woodland, vlei margins, vleis or rocky ground on a wide range of soils.

Distribution Very widespread in Rhodesia except on high mountains and in arid lowveld. It is found in all provinces of South Africa, extending north to Guinea, Ethiopia and western Arabia.

General The flowers may be plain orange, red or yellow, or variously streaked or speckled in combinations of brown, orange, yellow and red. A distinctive cultivar which has late flowers is common in gardens in southern Africa, America and Australia, and is somewhat similar to plants from the coasts of Natal and Mozambique. The cultivated form differs from most wild plants in producing numerous small corms, each on the end of an underground runner; wild plants normally produce numerous offset corms at the base of the parent corm. The disturbance of these corms during ploughing often makes this flower a common sight on arable lands in the eastern Tribal Trust areas of Rhodesia.

With such a wide distribution it is not surprising that this is a very variable species and that some of the extremes, for example, *G. psittacinus, G. primulinus* and *G. quartinianus,* were described as distinct species; they cannot, however, be kept separate from *G. natalensis.*

G. natalensis is one of the parents of the large-flowered commercial *Gladiolus* hybrids. The clear yellow-flowered species from the Victoria Falls (originally known as *G. primulinus*) was introduced to horticulture in 1902, and from it breeders were able to develop new hybrids and cultivars.

22 Anomatheca grandiflora Bak. *Plate* 41

large painted-petals

Family Iridaceae

Synonym *Lapeirousia grandiflora*

Flowers December to February.

Habitat Rocky ground in woodland, on granite and schists, in higher rainfall areas.

Distribution Widespread in Rhodesia, occurring on the central watershed extending to the edge of the Zambezi escarpment, south to Chibi and Bikita and west to the Matopos. To the north it reaches Zambia, Malawi and Tanzania and extends as far south as parts of Natal and the Transvaal.

General The genus *Anomatheca* has recently been resurrected to include five species that had for a long time been included in *Lapeirousia*. These five species have a round-based corm covered by a tunic of fine fibres clearly derived from the leaf bases. The corms of *Lapeirousia* are covered by hard woody entire tunics. These distinctions between the two genera are backed up by significant cytological differences.

A. grandiflora is distinguished from its nearest relative *A. laxa* (painted-petals) by its perianth segments which are longer than the tube and are held in the form of a cup, and not at right angles to the tube. The showy flowers are 3 to 4 cm in diameter with the tube distinctly wider at the throat than in *A. laxa*. The distribution of the two species overlaps in southern Mozambique and Zululand, but *A. laxa* has not been recorded from Rhodesia. Both species have been successfully cultivated. They reproduce readily from the attractive shiny orange seeds that are revealed when the fruiting capsule splits open.

The meaning of *Anomatheca* is 'anomalous capsule' and this refers to the wart-like papillae that cover the fruiting capsule and which were originally regarded as an important and unusual feature.

Plate 42   Plate 43

23 Lapeirousia odoratissima Bak.

Plate 42

rhodesian spider-lily

Family Iridaceae

Flowers December to February.

Habitat Short open grassland on granite sandveld and in woodland on Kalahari Sand.

Distribution Widely distributed in Rhodesia; extends from Zaire and Tanzania southwards to Rhodesia, Zambia, Angola and South West Africa.

General The creamy white star-shaped flowers are up to 10 cm across and have a tube measuring up to 15 cm long.

The genus *Lapeirousia* is confined to tropical and South Africa and contains quite a large number of species of which nineteen occur in the winter rainfall area of South Africa and about six or seven in Rhodesia.

One other species, *L. schimperi*, is obviously related to *L. odoratissima* but is taller and has a branched inflorescence. It occurs in woodland on sand in the northern and western parts of the country. To the casual observer the other Rhodesian species of *Lapeirousia* would not appear to be closely related.

The specific name of *L. odoratissima* refers to the sweet scent of the flowers, most noticeable in the evening. The common name has come into use because of a superficial resemblance to species of *Hymenocallis* commonly cultivated in gardens or in pots.

From early in the nineteenth century until recently *Lapeirousia* was misspelled *Lapeyrousia*; however the genus was named by Pourret after his friend, Baron de la Peirouse, a naturalist who was an expert on the flora of the Pyrenees.

24 Moraea spathulata (L.f.) Klatt

Plate 43

large yellow tulp

Family Iridaceae

Flowers December to March.

Habitat Open grassland and on stream banks and mountainsides at altitudes of at least 2 000 m.

Distribution Inyanga and Melsetter districts in Rhodesia, extending southwards via the eastern Transvaal along the slopes of the Drakensberg mountains to the eastern Cape.

General At first glance a species of *Moraea* looks very similar to an iris, and it has recently been suggested that *Dietes*, a genus that has one species in the forests of eastern Rhodesia, may be the common ancestor of *Iris* and *Moraea*. However, they differ in that the root-stock of *Iris* has remained a rhizome or been modified to a bulb, whereas in *Moraea* the root-stock is a corm, and the flowers of *Iris* have a perianth tube, a feature which is absent in *Moraea* except in one species; furthermore, *Iris* is a genus of the northern hemisphere, whereas *Moraea* is an African genus containing some sixty species which occur mainly south of the equator.

About seven species of *Moraea* occur in Rhodesia. A smaller yellow-flowered, apparently undescribed, species occurs on Mount Inyangani. All the other species have blue flowers, often with yellow guide markings. The two most common are *M. carsonii* and *M. schimperi;* the former is a small-flowered plant of grassland and is particularly common in soil pockets on granite, while the latter has flowers about 5 cm in diameter and is rather localised along stream banks and the edges of vleis in the highveld. Both these species and *M. spathulata* are toxic to stock and probably cause an appreciable number of cattle deaths each year; in fact all species of *Moraea* should be regarded as being potentially poisonous.

Plate 44

Plate 45

25 Oenostachys zambesiacus (Bak.) Goldblatt

Plate 44

zambezi wine-spike

Family   Iridaceae

Flowers   January to March

Habitat   In glades in *Baikiaea plurijuga* (rhodesian teak) woodland on deep Kalahari Sand at about 1 200 m above sea level.

Distribution   From Nyamandhlovu to Victoria Falls in the western part of Rhodesia, extending into southern Zambia and along the Chobe river in northern Botswana.

General   This species would be an attractive and interesting garden plant. The flower spikes are up to 1,2 m tall and make a striking sight in the endless greens and browns of the dense woodland in which the plants are found. The Kalahari Sand on which they grow is up to 100 m deep and is very fine grained. Although porous and infertile it supports a surprisingly luxuriant and varied woodland flora.

Oenostachys is fairly closely related to *Gladiolus* but it differs in that the upper segment of the perianth is elongated and hood-like. The first *Oenostachys* was described from Mount Elgon in Uganda; it had large wine coloured bracts which almost hid the flowers. The generic name, which directly translated means 'wine-spike', refers to these showy bracts. It has since been realised that most of the species previously referred to the South African genus *Petamenes* are better placed in *Oenostachys*.

O. zambesiacus was first collected in 1883 by Dr Emil Holub, the Austrian explorer, in the Leshumo valley which is in the Matetsi area on the border between Rhodesia and Botswana. It was described by Baker as *Antholyza zambesiaca*.

26 Kaempferia decora Van Druten

Plate 45

yellow ginger

Family   Zingiberaceae

Flowers   November to January.

Habitat   Mostly at low altitudes in woodland areas of high rainfall and lush vegetation.

Distribution   In Rhodesia in suitable localities along the Mozambique border from the Holdenby Tribal Trust Land to Mount Selinda. It is also recorded from Zambia, Tanzania, Malawi and Mozambique.

General   This species was first described in 1953 from specimens collected at Garuso in Mozambique some sixty-five km east of Umtali. Its flowers are among the most attractive in a genus noted for its beauty, and the specific name, meaning 'pretty', is well deserved. The plants produce canna-like leaves 20 to 40 cm long simultaneously with the flowers. The flowers open singly in succession but each individual flower lasts for only one day. The roots are fleshy and arise from a short rhizome. It would be worth growing as a pot plant and would require a rich acid soil with adequate leaf mould and shade.

Besides the three species of *Kaempferia* dealt with in this book, a further species, *K. rhodesica*, deserves mention. This is a white night-flowering species which is very widespread in Zambia; it has a very brief flowering period. Despite its specific name it has not been found in Rhodesia, but should be looked for along the Zambezi escarpment.

The genus *Kaempferia* was named after Engelbert Kaempfer (1651-1716), a German physician who collected plants in Asia, where many of the sixty or so species of *Kaempferia* occur.

Plate 46

Plate 48

Plate 47

27 Kaempferia aethiopica (Solms-Laub.) Benth. Plate 46

mauve ginger

Family Zingiberaceae

Flowers November to December.

Habitat Woodland, often in fairly high rainfall areas and at low altitudes.

Distribution In the Zambezi valley and the lower lying more humid valleys of eastern Rhodesia. Occurs from Senegal to Ethiopia southwards to Angola, Rhodesia and Mozambique.

General *K. aethiopica* has spectacular flowers that occur in pairs at ground level, usually well before the leaves appear. Veld fires encourage the plant to flower and it is then, when all the surrounding vegetation has been burned down, that mauve ginger is seen at its best. In Rhodesia it is a fairly local plant, but if one has travelled through the woodlands of Zambia just before or during the early rains, these flowers are a very familiar sight.

The most obvious and largest floral organ is the conspicuous mauve lip which one would suppose to be a petal, but which is actually thought to be derived from the fusion of three stamens. The three true petals are joined to form a tube below and are insignificant by comparison. Several sets of flowers are produced in succession and when they die down the relatively large leaves come up. The roots are fleshy and smell of ginger. The tall wild gingers growing in the forests in the east of Rhodesia belong to the related genus *Aframomum*.

28 Kaempferia rosea Schweinf. ex Benth. & Hook.f.

rose ginger Plates 47 and 48

Family Zingiberaceae

Synonym *K. carsonii*

Flowers November to January.

Habitat On a wide variety of soils; often in semi-shade in rich soils in woodland; sometimes at the base of termite mounds.

Distribution Throughout the northern half of Rhodesia, from Wankie to Shamva and south to Beatrice and Hartley. It extends northwards through eastern Africa to the Sudan.

General This species is the most widely distributed member of the genus in Rhodesia and is one of the country's most attractive flowers. Plants are easily transplanted or grown from seed, and produce a succession of flowers over a period of two weeks or more. The flower spike is 20 to 30 cm tall and each flower is about 6 cm across. As in the preceding two species, the apparent petal is derived from modified sterile stamens. The large central lobe or lip sometimes has a deep maroon blotch on either side of the yellow guide marking. As is usual in this family, the petals are relatively inconspicuous.

Zingiber officinale also belongs to the Zingiberaceae and is the source of commercial ginger; it is widely cultivated by Africans in the Melsetter and Chipinga districts where it is used medicinally, principally as a cure for constipation. It is also sold as a medicine in African markets in urban areas. *Curcuma domestica* (turmeric) also belongs to the ginger family. Turmeric is used to give the yellow colour and musky flavour to curry powder. It is grown mainly in India and countries of south-eastern Asia.

Plate 49   Plate 50

var. **nilotica** (Bak.) Summerh.

leopard orchid; mopane orchid

Family   Orchidaceae

Flowers   September to November.

Habitat   Epiphytic on trees in various types of woodland.

Distribution   Widespread in Rhodesia except at the highest altitudes; it extends northwards to Nigeria and Kenya and southwards to southern Mozambique and the Transvaal.

General   *A. gigantea* var. *nilotica* is the best known and largest of the epiphytes that occur in Rhodesia. The number and variety of epiphytic orchids is greater in tropical than in subtropical or temperate countries, thus Rhodesia, with eighty-five species of epiphytic orchids, has twice as many as South Africa.

     A. gigantea var. *gigantea* has smaller flowers which are less heavily marked with large brown spots and more round in outline than are the elongated flowers of var. *nilotica*. It flowers from May to September and occurs in the Transvaal, Swaziland, Mozambique and northern Natal. The two varieties are indistinguishable except when they are in flower and even then are not always readily separable.

     The leopard orchid is used by Africans for a surprising number of purposes including the prevention of diarrhoea, as an aphrodisiac, as a good luck charm and to prevent pigeons from flying. In areas of urban development and near main roads it is much less common than formerly because of its desirability as a garden plant. It is now one of the specially protected indigenous plants scheduled under the Parks and Wild Life Act.

     The genus *Ansellia* was named after Mr Ansell of the Horticultural Society of London who was associated with Dr Vogel on the 1841 Niger expedition.

tassel orchid

Family   Orchidaceae

Flowers   October and November.

Habitat   Open grassland and hilly *Brachystegia* woodland, especially on granite sandveld.

Distribution   On the central watershed from Umtali and Inyanga to Salisbury. Occurs also on the Transvaal highveld and is recorded from Tanzania.

General   It is most surprising to encounter such a delicate orchid in full flower, baking in the dry veld under an October sun before the rains have broken. The one to two fleshy basal leaves which lie flat on the ground and are up to 4 to 7 cm in diameter have usually withered and often completely disappeared before the flowering season. The flowering stems are about 30 cm tall and the flowers larger than those of most other members of the genus. The fine marginal dissections of the petals and lip are characteristic of the genus and, in *H. randii*, make the flowers look rather like teased out pieces of cotton-wool caught on erect stems.

     Out of a genus with a total of fifty-five species, all of which occur in Africa or Arabia, only five species are to be found in Rhodesia. The other four species are comparatively uncommon, as well as being relatively small and inconspicuous; they occur in the mountains of the eastern districts.

     The generic name means 'whole hair' and evidently refers to the hairiness of the type species. *H. randii* is named after Dr Richard Frank Rand (1856-1937) who, as a medical officer to the British South Africa Company, travelled with the pioneer column from Macloutsie to Salisbury. He became Salisbury's first general practitioner.

Plate 51   Plate 52

31 Disa ochrostachya Reichenb.f.   *Plate* 51

golden candle orchid

Family Orchidaceae

Flowers January and February.

Habitat Montane grassland and vleis.

Distribution Very local on the eastern border mountains from Inyanga to Chipinga, and in the Makoni district; extending west to Angola and northwards to Cameroun and Kenya.

General The striking yellow flower spikes with their rusty orange to reddish markings, especially on the hooded dorsal sepal, readily catch the eye in the short green grass among the heaths and everlastings on the Inyanga Downs. The plants may be as tall as 1,3 m with an inflorescence of up to 40 cm.

If a wide concept of *Disa* is taken and *Herschelia* is included, this genus can be said to consist of about one hundred and thirty species. Most of these occur in Africa with four recorded from the Malagasy Republic and the Mascarene Islands, and over eighty recorded from South Africa. *Disa* is characterised by an erect hooded dorsal sepal which usually has a single spur. The lip is lowermost but is not usually as prominent a feature in this genus as is the dorsal sepal.

The red disa, *D. uniflora*, which occurs in the mountains of the south-western Cape, is the best known species, having exceptionally large flowers for the genus. *D. ornithantha* is found in the mountains of eastern Rhodesia and has red flowers similar in form to those of *D. uniflora* but much smaller. Some twenty species of *Disa* occur in Rhodesia.

The derivation of the generic name is obscure. The specific name *ochrostachya* means 'yellow flower spike'.

32 Disa versicolor Reichenb.f.   *Plate* 52

variable disa

Family Orchidaceae

Flowers December to March.

Habitat Montane grassland and vlei, often among rocks.

Distribution Mountains of eastern Rhodesia from the Inyanga Downs to the Chimanimani mountains, extending into Mozambique and southwards via the Drakensberg mountains to the eastern Cape.

General The flowers are variously described as pink, purple, cerise or red. As they age they turn yellow or greenish and it is this change of colour, which is not always apparent in all populations, that has given rise to the specific name. The showy, tightly clustered flowers make a brilliant splash of colour in the green grass. Each plant grows from paired tubers, the flower being produced from the older one. The leaves grow from a sterile shoot.

All of the twenty Rhodesian species of *Disa* have colourful flowers. *D. hamatopetala* is a blue-flowered species which can be alternatively placed in the genus *Herschelia*. It is a fine sight in September and October in the montane grassland of the Inyanga and Melsetter districts and elsewhere. *D. equestris*, a violet-flowered species, is locally common in wetter vleis. *D. walleri* is a comparatively rare species of wet vleis and has large purple flowers conspicuously spotted with dark purple.

As with most of the grassland, vlei and swamp orchids, it is futile for the enthusiastic gardener to attempt to transplant this species as it will certainly die. The specialised damp conditions it requires cannot be reproduced in the average garden. It should be left in the wild for all to enjoy.

Plate 53 Plate 54

33 Eulophia cucullata (Sw. ex Pers.) Steud. *Plate 53*

foxglove orchid

Family Orchidaceae

Synonym *Lissochilus arenarius*

Flowers November to January.

Habitat Woodland and vlei margins.

Distribution Widespread throughout Rhodesia in suitable habitats and in all neighbouring countries except Botswana. In South Africa it is confined to coastal Natal. It extends up eastern Africa as far as the Sudan, west to Angola and Zaire, and from Nigeria to Gambia.

General This is one of the most common and attractive of all African ground orchids. Its flowers, 25 to 30 mm in diameter, are astonishingly variable in size and colour and can be sweetly scented or completely lacking in fragrance. The leaves are stiff and grass–like and appear after the flowers.

Three of the commoner and more spectacular early flowering woodland species of *Eulophia* are the pure yellow-flowered *E. speciosa*, the mauve-flowered *E. livingstoniana*, which is frequently found in association with *E. speciosa*, and the brown and yellow-flowered *E. streptopetala* which may be 2 m in height. The leaves of all these species appear after the flowers.

The genus *Eulophia* takes its name from the Greek for 'well developed crest', a reference to the crest on the lip which is present in most species. The specific name means 'hooded', and is derived from the short rounded spur which resembles a monk's cowl or hood.

Africans in Malawi use the tubers to give a slimy consistency to certain dishes.

This species is one of the specially protected indigenous plants scheduled under the Parks and Wild Life Act.

34 Eulophia zeyheri Hook.f. *Plate 54*

banana orchid

Family Orchidaceae

Flowers November and December.

Habitat *Brachystegia* and other types of woodland, often among rocks and in grassland or on vlei margins.

Distribution Scattered along the eastern border in suitable habitats from Inyanga to Chipinga, being especially common in the Chipinga area and along the central watershed to Selukwe and Matopos. In the north it extends to Malawi and East Africa, although so far it is not known in Zambia, and to the south it reaches the Transkei via the Transvaal and the Natal highveld.

General Before the buds open the flower head resembles a miniature bunch of ripe bananas. There is a tendency for the Rhodesian plants to have deeper yellow flowers than do those from South Africa. There is also some variation in the colour of the blotch on the lip; in the Transkei this is a series of crimson veins, in the Transvaal the veins are dull maroon and somewhat suffused, and in Rhodesia the plants have an orange or chestnut brown blotch on the lip at the throat.

This species has been regarded by some authors as indistinguishable from the orange-flowered *E. welwitschii*. However, until more evidence is forthcoming, it would seem best to consider the two species as being distinct.

About seventy species of *Eulophia* occur in Rhodesia, making it by far the largest genus of orchids in the country. All the species are terrestrial, some being adapted to dry woodland while others flourish in the wettest of vleis. The flowers vary greatly in size and colour.

The species was named after a German, C. L. P. Zeyher (1799-1868), who arrived in South Africa in 1822 where, for many years, he made his living as a plant collector.

Plate 55

Plate 56

35 Satyrium longicauda Lindl. *Plate 55*

blushing bride satyrium

Family Orchidaceae

Flowers January to April.

Habitat Grassy mountainsides and amongst rocks at altitudes above 2 000 m where mist and drizzle may occur at any time throughout the year.

Distribution In Rhodesia on the eastern mountains from Inyanga south to the Chimanimanis. Occurs also in southern Tanzania, Malawi and Mozambique, extending to the eastern Cape via eastern Transvaal and the Drakensberg mountains in Natal.

General *Satyrium* is a genus containing over a hundred species, most of which have been recorded from southern Africa. Nineteen of these occur in Rhodesia, of which a number have quite striking flowers. In many genera of orchids the ovary is twisted through a one hundred and eighty degree angle, with the result that the lip is lowermost. However, in *Satyrium* the lip is at the top of the flower and is unusual in that it is hooded and possesses two long tails or spurs. Some species of *Disa* are superficially similar to *Satyrium* but in the former the single-spurred hood is the odd sepal, and the lip is at the bottom of the flower.

The flowers of *S. longicauda* may be pure white, variously tinged with pink, or variegated with purple. The flower stem is covered by sheathing leaves decreasing in size the higher they occur on the stem. Another short stem bearing three to five leaves but no flowers arises alongside the flowering stem.

A closely related species, *S. buchananii*, has rather similar but larger flowers with longer spurs; it occurs in vleis in the north-western and central areas of Rhodesia.

Dioscorides used the name Satyrion for one of the orchids, evidently in allusion to its reputed aphrodisiac properties. The specific name means 'long-tailed'.

36 Satyrium neglectum Schlechter *Plate 56*

pink candle satyrium

Family Orchidaceae

Flowers February to April.

Habitat Montane grassland above 2 000 m.

Distribution In suitable habitats from the southern highlands of Tanzania, south through Malawi and Mozambique to the eastern Cape via the Drakensberg mountains.

General The flowers of the Rhodesian form of *S. neglectum* are fragrant and vary from pale to rich carmine pink. This species is obviously allied to *S. longicauda* and possesses the same type of sterile leaf-bearing shoot from a separate bud at the base of the flowering stem.

The specific name means 'overlooked' or 'insignificant'.

Some of the other species of *Satyrium* found in Rhodesia are very different in appearance and occur in different habitats: *S. anomalum* is a plant of *Brachystegia* woodland and has greenish flowers tinged with red or purple with the twin spurs curved upwards, somewhat like a snail's horns; *S. trinerve* (*S. atherstonei*) is a common species from vlei and wet grassland and has white flowers with yellow on the lip, and white and green bracts that give colour to the inflorescence; *S. breve*, with its short compact pink inflorescence, occurs on mountains from Inyanga to the Chimanimanis.

In Rhodesia there are over three hundred and thirty species of orchids belonging to fifty-three genera, therefore it is inevitable that several important genera have had to be omitted from this book. These include *Brachycorythis*, which has seven species in Rhodesia, all with attractive flowers; *Habenaria*, containing fifty-seven Rhodesian species which have green or white flowers, and which occur in vleis and woodland; and *Platycoryne*, containing four Rhodesian species which have bright orange or pale yellow flowers.

Plate 57

Plate 58

Plate 59

37 Protea angolensis Welw.   *Plates* 57 *and* 58

var. **angolensis** (Plate 57)

var. **divaricata** (Engl. & Gilg) Beard (Plate 58)

angolan protea

Family   Proteaceae

Synonym   *P. chionantha*

Flowers   January to July. Var. *angolensis* tends to flower between January and March and var. *divaricata* tends to flower between April and July, but there is some overlap.

Habitat   Var. *angolensis* favours open grassland or the marginal grassland found in the transitional zone between vlei and woodland. Var. *divaricata* occurs mainly in *Brachystegia* woodland.

Distribution   Var. *angolensis* is most common on the central watershed in Rhodesia from Gwelo to Rusape. It extends westwards to Angola and northwards to Zaire and southern Tanzania. Var. *divaricata* is rather more widespread, extending within Rhodesia from Umtali to Banket and Sipolilo. It is widely dispersed with much the same distribution outside Rhodesia as var. *angolensis*.

General   The species is divided into two varieties: var. *angolensis*, a dwarf plant with numerous unbranched stems up to 50 cm tall which die back or are burned back to ground level each year; and var. *divaricata* which develops into a small tree 2 to 4 m in height. This tree can be distinguished from *P. gaguedi* (*P. abyssinica*) by its rather wider leaves. It seems possible that the two varieties may in fact be worth specific rank, since they grow together without any apparent intermediates.

There are some one hundred and thirty species of *Protea*, all of which occur in tropical and South Africa. Nine species are found in Rhodesia. The great diversity of form and flower colour in the genus led to its being called after Proteus, the Greek sea god who could assume many guises. The specific name means 'from Angola'.

38 Protea gazensis Beard   *Plate* 59

manica protea

Family   Proteaceae

Flowers   October to April but mainly in January and February.

Habitat   Woodland in valleys and on hillsides in higher rainfall areas. Sometimes in open grassland with scattered ericoid shrubs.

Distribution   From Inyanga to Melsetter and the Chimanimani mountains, and on Gorongosa mountain in Mozambique.

General   A very attractive species closely allied to *P. caffra* and *P. rhodantha* from the Transvaal. The plant ranges in size from bushes 2 m tall to trees 5 m tall; it tends to be shorter in more exposed situations. The flower heads and clusters of bright red young leaves are very showy. Proteas differ from pincushions (*Leucospermum*) in that the flower heads are surrounded by large bracts which are often brightly coloured. Each flower head is composed of a large number of densely packed individual flowers.

Besides the widespread species (mentioned under *P. welwitschii*), there are four other species in Rhodesia which are found only in the eastern districts, two being endemic to the Inyanga area and two to the Chimanimani mountains. *P. inyanganiensis*, which is a dwarf shrub forming compact clumps up to 80 cm tall, is known only from the summit of Inyangani mountain. *P. asymmetrica* is also a rare species in the Inyanga area; it reaches over 1,5 m in height and is so called because its flower heads develop asymmetrically. *P. neocrinita* is a white-flowered species; it grows on the Chimanimani mountains at an altitude of about 1 500 m, reaching heights of up to 1,3 m. *P. enervis* is a small plant with annual branches which lie prostrate on the white quartzite sands of the Chimanimani mountains; it is quite the most distinctive of the Rhodesian proteas.

Plate 60

Plate 61

39 Protea welwitschii Engl.   *Plate 60*

rusty velvet protea

Family Proteaceae

Synonym *P. hirta*

Flowers March to July.

Habitat *Brachystegia* woodland, sometimes on rocky hillsides and in grassland with scattered trees.

Distribution From Chipinga to Inyanga and along the watershed to Salisbury; on the Great Dyke and northwards to Zambia where it is common. It also extends south to the Transvaal and Natal, and north to Zaire and Tanzania.

General This species is normally a shrub up to 2 m tall, but in high cool sites it tends to be shorter than this, and in more favourable locations may reach up to 5 m in height. Its hairy leaves serve to distinguish it from most other species. A number of subspecies have been described but they tend to grade into one another and it is best to regard *P. welwitschii* as a variable species without attempting infraspecific subdivision.

In Rhodesia there are only four species of *Protea* that are widespread: *P. angolensis*, *P. welwitschii*, *P. gaguedi* and *P. petiolaris*. *P. gaguedi*, with its creamy white flowers and relatively narrow leaves, is the most widely distributed of all tropical proteas. It was described from Ethiopia and, in fact, *gaguedi* is an Ethiopian vernacular name. Its north/south range extends from Ethiopia to Natal and it reaches Angola in the west. *P. petiolaris* occurs in *Brachystegia* woodland and grassland at higher altitudes. It reaches Tanzania to the north and Angola to the west.

P. welwitschii is named in honour of Dr Friedrich Welwitsch (1806-1872), the Austrian explorer and botanist who collected in Angola between 1853 and 1860. His collection was more prolific and better documented than any compiled until that date, and indeed it surpasses most collections that have been made since.

40 Leucospermum saxosum S. Moore   *Plate 61*

chimanimani pincushion

Family Proteaceae

Flowers Throughout the year with a peak period in the spring from September to December.

Habitat Rocky ground among quartzite outcrops in montane grassland.

Distribution Chimanimani mountains on both the Rhodesian and Mozambique sides, and in the Drakensberg mountains of the eastern Transvaal.

General The flower heads are about 8 cm across and are quite the most conspicuous and colourful constituents of the vegetation amongst the weirdly eroded lichen-covered grey quartzite rocks of the Chimanimani mountains. The bushes average about 1 m in height.

The pincushions are close relatives of the proteas and, like them, are very much a feature of the winter rainfall area of the southern and south-western Cape. In fact, forty-three out of forty-seven species contained in the genus are confined to this area. *L. saxosum* is the northern-most representative of the genus and is evidence of a link, at some time in the past, between the flora of the Rhodesian and South African mountain ranges. *L. saxosum* is closely related to the other three species, *L. cuneiforme*, *L. innovans*, and *L. gerrardii*, whose range is outside or extends outside the winter rainfall area.

Leucospermum means 'white seed' and *saxosum* means 'rocky'.

Plate 62

Plate 63

41 Loranthus braunii Engl. *Plate 62*

crimson mistletoe

Family Loranthaceae

Synonym *Globimetula braunii*

Flowers June to September.

Habitat Parasitic on a number of wild trees, for example, *Ficus*, *Protea* and *Strychnos*, but apparently not particular about its host. It is a common pest in orchards and also attacks other exotic trees, such as *Callistemon*, *Morus*, *Bauhinia*, *Annona* and *Acacia*.

Distribution Widely distributed in the highveld of Rhodesia, being particularly abundant in the Salisbury area. Also from Ghana to Tanzania and south to Angola.

General This is a most striking species with its massed deep crimson flowers making a vivid splash of colour in the trees in winter.

Loranthus has been split into a number of different genera in recent years. However, it is considered best to retain it as a single genus at present, with the floral differences allowing it to be split into sections rather than genera. In the new classification *L. braunii* was placed under *Globimetula*.

All African Loranthaceae are parasites and both *Viscum* and *Loranthus* are commonly referred to as mistletoe. The plants are spread by birds which eat the berries and then wipe the sticky seeds off their beaks against a branch. Here the seeds germinate and, where the root touches the bark, a disc or callus is formed from which strands arise and penetrate the branch to tap the sap stream of the host tree.

Loranthus means 'strap flower'.

42 Loranthus curviflorus Benth. ex Oliv. *Plate 63*

acacia mistletoe

Family Loranthaceae

Synonyms *Loranthus kalachariensis; Plicosepalus curviflorus*

Flowers May to September, but may be found in flower at almost any time of the year.

Habitat Parasitic mainly on species of *Acacia*, but may occur also on *Albizia*, *Dichrostachys* and *Brachystegia*, or more rarely on species of non-leguminous genera such as *Commiphora* or *Carissa*.

Distribution It is widely distributed throughout Rhodesia, but is more common at low altitudes in the low to moderate rainfall areas and is absent from the high rainfall areas of the eastern mountains. It is found in Egypt, Arabia, the Sudan and Ethiopia southwards to South West Africa, Botswana, the Transvaal and Natal.

General This is one of the most common and widespread of the species of *Loranthus*. It is particularly partial to parasitising *Acacia karroo*, and indeed there sometimes seems to be more parasite than host tree, the drooping masses of *Loranthus* making the crown of the *Acacia* appear to be ablaze with pink. Members of the genus *Loranthus* usually have joined petals, but *L. curviflorus* and one other species are the only two out of twenty to thirty Rhodesian species that have free petals. As the specific name suggests the flowers are curved.

Various species of *Loranthus* are the food plants of the brilliant blue sapphire butterflies, *Iolaus* (family Lycaenidae). The pupa of one species, *Iolaus sidus*, closely resembles a germinating *Loranthus* seed — a most extraordinary case of protective mimicry.

Plate 64

Plate 65

Plate 66

43 Talinum arnotii Hook.f. *Plate 64*

kalahari butterweed

Family Portulacaceae

Flowers December to January.

Habitat In Rhodesia it occurs on sandy soils in areas of low rainfall where acacias and baobabs are dominant.

Distribution In Rhodesia it is recorded from the Sabi valley, Chiredzi and Beitbridge. It occurs also in Zambia, but is most common in Botswana and South West Africa, and extends into the northern Cape, the Orange Free State and the Transvaal.

General In a good rainy season this plant forms extensive patches on roadsides and bare ground. The deep butter yellow flowers contrast well with the bright green foliage, which is eaten as a spinach or salad by the local African people.

Four other species of *Talinum* occur wild in Rhodesia. *T. portulacifolium* has pink or mauve flowers and is up to a metre in height. The other three species are all yellow-flowered and difficult to distinguish from *T. arnotii*: *T. caffrum*, a widespread species, has seeds with concentric ridges and narrower leaves; equally widespread is *T. tenuissimum* which has thread-like flower stalks and linear leaves; *T. crispatulum*, with its crisped leaf margins, is common in Botswana but only just extends into the west of Rhodesia.

The flowers of the yellow-flowered species open for only a single afternoon and close at dusk.

The origin of the generic name is obscure; it has been suggested that it is derived from an African vernacular name. The species is named after David Arnot who lived in Griqualand West during the nineteenth century, and who helped to secure the diamond fields in that area for the Cape government. He was a keen plant collector and has several species named in his honour.

44 Nymphaea petersiana Klotzsch *Plates 65 and 66*

lowveld waterlily

Family Nymphaeaceae

Flowers Throughout the year if water is available, but especially February to May.

Habitat Perennial or seasonal pans and pools in slow flowing streams, mainly at low altitudes.

Distribution Wherever suitable habitats are available in the Sabi, Limpopo, Zambezi and other river valleys; also extending into the Transvaal, Angola, Zambia, Malawi, Mozambique and Tanzania.

General The delicate blue flowers, which are thrust slightly above the water, are of universal appeal. Unfortunately it is not possible to capture the exact shade of blue of this and other blue flowers in a colour photograph.

N. petersiana is very similar to *N. capensis* as both have leaves with toothed margins. However, the latter has the closed network of ribbed veins on the lower surface of the leaf extending more than two-thirds of the way towards the margin. *N. capensis*, while occurring in surrounding countries, is apparently somewhat uncommon in Rhodesia, having been recorded only from the Urungwe district.

The most common waterlily in Rhodesia is *N. caerulea*. It also has pale bluish flowers, but its leaf margins are not toothed. The white flowered *N. lotus* with its sharply toothed leaves is a plant of deep permanent pools and rivers. The presence of waterlilies indicates a suitable habitat for the species of snail which may carry bilharzia.

The generic name means 'sacred to the nymphs'; the latter were Greek goddesses of lower rank who presided over springs and streams. The species was named after Dr W. C. Peters, a German who collected in the Zambezi province of Mozambique from 1843 to 1847.

Plate 67

Plate 68

Plate 69

45 Clematis brachiata Thunb. *Plates 67 and 68*

travellers' joy

Family Ranunculaceae

Flowers February to May.

Habitat In woodland and wooded grassland; it often grows at the base of granite hills.

Distribution It occurs throughout most of Rhodesia except at low altitudes; it is widely distributed in tropical and South Africa from Senegal to the Cape, but is absent in the winter rainfall regions of the Cape, and is not found in areas of semi-desert or the high rainfall forests of the tropics.

General This is a woody climber which, in autumn, covers the supporting bushes and trees with masses of sweetly scented flowers; in winter the persistent white feathery styles of the fruits continue to be a conspicuous sight. The petiole and rachis of the compound leaves act as tendrils and twine round twigs giving additional support to the climbing stems, which can reach the tops of the tallest trees.

The generic name *Clematis* is derived from the Greek word for a vine; the specific name *brachiata* means literally 'with arms', but botanically it has a more exact application and refers to the fact that each succeeding pair of opposite leaves or branches is produced at right angles to the last.

There are some two hundred and fifty species of *Clematis* recorded mostly from temperate regions. The common name, traveller's joy, refers to *Clematis vitalba* which occurs in Britain — our plant is so close in appearance to the British plant that it has acquired the same name.

Three other species of *Clematis* occur in Rhodesia. The most familiar of these, *C. welwitschii*, is a short trailing perennial, seldom climbing and common in *Brachystegia* woodland in the highveld.

46 Clematopsis scabiosifolia (DC.) Hutch. *Plate 69*

shock-headed peter

Family Ranunculaceae

Flowers Late December to February.

Habitat *Brachystegia* woodland and grassland, not below about 1 000 m.

Distribution Throughout Rhodesia except at low altitudes, and generally distributed in tropical Africa, extending northwards to Nigeria and the Sudan and southwards to the Transvaal.

General This is a herbaceous perennial about a metre in height with drooping flowers which are normally creamy white but are sometimes tinted with mauve. After blooming the plant continues to be attractive as the spent flowers become erect and develop into fluffy white seed heads. Each seed has a silky feathery tail (the persistent style) which aids in its dispersal by the wind.

C. scabiosifolia is the only species of *Clematopsis* to occur in Rhodesia. It is very variable over its whole range, and even in Rhodesia the extremes look very different. For example, in the Kalahari Sand areas of Rhodesia its leaves tend to be much more dissected and have narrower divisions than those of the plants occurring in the rest of the country. Populations of similar plants are found in Zambia, Botswana and the Transvaal, but such is the variation that it seems best not to assign names to each of these elements, and rather to regard the whole as a very polymorphic species.

It seems very likely that *Clematopsis* has recently evolved from *Clematis* as an adaptation to the frequent fires in wooded and open grassland. Indeed *Clematopsis* is known to hybridise in nature with *Clematis brachiata* in the highveld of the Transvaal.

Clematopsis means 'like *Clematis*' and *scabiosifolia* means 'with leaves like a scabious'.

Plate 70   Plate 71

47 Cleome angustifolia Forsk.

Plate 70

subsp. **petersiana** (Klotzsch) Kers

yellow cleome; yellow mouse-whiskers

Family Capparaceae

Synonym *Cleome diandra*

Flowers November to June depending on the time of germination.

Habitat Occurs at low altitudes in low rainfall areas in mopane and other types of woodland. It often grows on disturbed sandy soils and, although it is frequently found in old lands, it is not a serious weed.

Distribution In Rhodesia it occurs in the lower and drier areas, especially in the Zambezi, Limpopo and Sabi river valleys. It occurs also in Niger, Ethiopia and Sudan and in the drier parts of Kenya and Tanzania, but its main areas of distribution are in south tropical Africa southwards to South West Africa, the northern part of the Cape Province, the Transvaal and Natal.

General These plants are slender erect annuals which may reach 1,6 m but are more often about 1 m in height or less depending upon the fertility of the soil in which they are growing.

C. angustifolia is readily distinguished from the other six species that occur in Rhodesia by its pretty yellow flowers with their violet-based unequal petals. There are no other yellow-flowered species in Rhodesia, although there is one that occurs in Botswana. The two large erect yellow petals and the reddish upturned filaments of the stamens make the common name an appropriate one. The leaflets are very narrow, being almost thread-like, and presumably help to protect the plant from drought by reducing the area of leaf capable of losing moisture through transpiration.

The origin of the name *Cleome* is obscure; the specific name *angustifolia* means 'narrow leaved' and the subspecies is named after the German botanist, Dr W. C. Peters, who collected in Mozambique in the mid-nineteenth century.

48 Cleome hirta (Klotzsch) Oliv.

Plate 71

sticky purple cleome

Family Capparaceae

Flowers January to May.

Habitat Mopane, mnondo and other types of woodland; occurs also in fallow land, at roadsides and as a weed on disturbed ground.

Distribution Throughout the lower and drier parts of Rhodesia, extending across to South West Africa, southwards to the Transvaal and the northern Cape, and northwards to Zaire, Uganda, Kenya and Somalia.

General This is an erect much-branched annual herb. Its leaves and stems are covered with numerous gland-tipped hairs and are therefore very sticky. The plants are about 1,5 m tall and are rounded in outline. The seed capsules of *Cleome* are long, thin and pod-like; those of *C. hirta* are up to 15 cm in length.

The leaves of some of the other species of *Cleome* (for example, *C. monophylla* and *C. gynandra*, both of which are relatively common weeds in Rhodesia) are used as a spinach by Africans. However, the leaves of *C. hirta* are not eaten as they are unpleasantly sticky and aromatic. The seeds of *C. hirta* are ground to a powder and used by Africans as a type of mustard.

The meaning of the specific name *hirta* is 'hairy'.

The family Capparaceae, the caper family, is named from the genus *Capparis* of which several species occur in Rhodesia. Capers are the pickled buds of *Capparis spinosa* which grows wild in the Mediterranean region. The other Rhodesian genera in the Capparaceae are all shrubs or trees and include *Boscia*, *Maerua* and *Cadaba*.

Plate 72

Plate 73

Plate 74

49 Dolichos kilimandscharicus Harms ex Taub.   *Plate* 72

veld lupin

Family Leguminosae; subfamily Papilionoideae

Synonyms *D. buchananii; D. lupiniflorus; D. malosanus*

Flowers September to November.

Habitat *Brachystegia* woodland and open grassland at medium to high altitudes.

Distribution From the top of the Zambezi escarpment along the central watershed to Hartley and across to Inyanga, thence down to Melsetter. It also extends via Enkeldoorn down to Fort Victoria but apparently is absent or at least scarce in Matabeleland. It extends southwards from the Sudan and Ethiopia to Angola, Rhodesia and Mozambique.

General This is an erect perennial herb extremely common over much of Mashonaland. It grows to over 1 m in height, the stems arising from a very large turnip-shaped root-stock which may be up to 30 cm in diameter. The mauve to light purple flowers look rather like certain cultivated lupins, but the resemblance is only superficial.

The root-stock looks red and meaty when cut; it is sometimes used as a fish poison and has shown some promise in the control of bilharzia.

The genus consists of about sixty species which have a mainly African distribution, although they do extend to India and eastern Asia. Several of the more familiar species have been transferred to other genera. *D. lablab* has become *Lablab purpureus*, and *D. axillaris*, together with all the related species of yellow-flowered climbing *Dolichos*, has been found to have tuberculate pollen and has now been placed in a separate genus, *Macrotyloma*.

Dolichos was a Greek word for bean; the specific name means 'from Mount Kilimanjaro', which is where the type specimen was collected.

50 Bauhinia galpinii N.E. Br.   *Plates* 73 and 74

red bauhinia

Family Leguminosae; subfamily Caesalpinioideae

Synonym *B. punctata*

Flowers November to March.

Habitat Dense woodland on hillsides and in riverine vegetation; often on termite mounds.

Distribution In Rhodesia, along the Zambezi escarpment and abundant in parts of the eastern districts at medium to low altitudes; occurring also in the Selukwe area and along the Lundi escarpment. It apparently does not occur north of the Zambezi and extends southwards into Mozambique, northern and eastern Transvaal, Swaziland and Zululand.

General The flowering period of this spectacular bush or scrambling shrub extends over several months. If suitable trees are available it can climb to 10 m or more, but it is normally a shrub 2 to 3 m in height. The pods are flat, brown and leathery and open explosively when ripe.

In cultivation it can be kept trimmed by being cut back after flowering. It grows readily from seed or cuttings and is a popular garden ornamental in Rhodesia and South Africa, as well as other parts of the world where climatic conditions are suitable. In South Africa *B. galpinii* is known as 'pride of de kaap' because it is very prevalent in the De Kaap valley near Barberton. As it is the only *Bauhinia* with brick red flowers in southern Africa it is unlikely to be confused with any other species. The pink and white *Bauhinia* that is most commonly cultivated as a garden and street tree in Rhodesia is *B. variegata*, which was introduced from India.

The species is named after Dr E. E. Galpin, a banker who was also a botanical enthusiast and who collected well and extensively in the Transvaal over many years.

Plate 75

Plate 76

Plate 77

51 Bauhinia macrantha Oliv.

Plate 75

rag bush; small white bauhinia

Family Leguminosae; subfamily Caesalpinioideae

Flowers October to January.

Habitat Deep well drained Kalahari Sand supporting woodland consisting of rhodesian teak (*Baikiaea plurijuga*), mukwa (*Pterocarpus angolensis*), mangwe (*Terminalia sericea*) and burkea (*Burkea africana*).

Distribution From the Bulawayo area to Victoria Falls, and eastwards on the plateau above the Zambezi escarpment down to the Lower Gwelo Tribal Trust Land. It extends through western Zambia and Botswana to South West Africa and southern Angola.

General This shrub grows from 1 to 2 m tall and is locally abundant wherever Kalahari Sand occurs in Matabeleland. The very delicate crimped white petals are soon dashed by rain and leave the bushes looking as though they are covered by innumerable bits of wrung-out wet rag. The petals tend to be wider than those of *B. petersiana*, and the shrub is normally much shorter in stature. The bilobed leaf is split down the centre for more than half the leaf length. It is hardly, if ever, found off Kalahari Sand.

In South West Africa the ripe beans are roasted and eaten. The leaves are browsed by cattle.

The genus is named after Jean and Caspar Bauhin, famous herbalists of the sixteenth century, because, according to Linnaeus, the two lobes recall the two brothers.

The specific name means 'large flowered'.

52 Bauhinia petersiana Bolle

Plates 76 and 77

large white bauhinia

Family Leguminosae; subfamily Caesalpinioideae

Flowers October to February.

Habitat Mixed woodland on a variety of soils at medium to low altitudes.

Distribution Northern and eastern Rhodesia. It extends northwards from Zambia, Rhodesia and Mozambique to Zaire and Tanzania.

General This species is superficially similar to *B. macrantha* but it does not occur on Kalahari Sand and it is usually a large bush or a small tree. Several other characters further distinguish it: the pubescence on the lower side of the leaf is of appressed hairs as opposed to the curved non-appressed ones of *B. macrantha;* the inflorescences are, to some extent, aggregated together instead of being scattered; the leaves are larger and are usually bilobed for less than halfway; the petals are narrower and the pods are wider than those of *B. macrantha*, and the flowers have conspicuous red filaments. Taken in isolation none of these characters would be enough to separate a species but there is no doubt about its distinctness. Occasionally, however, it is quite difficult to assign with complete certainty a given sprig of *Bauhinia* to its correct species.

The seeds of *B. petersiana* were roasted and ground as a coffee substitute by the early pioneers.

It is named after Dr Wilhelm Peters (1815-1883), a German botanist, who collected in Mozambique in the Zambezi province.

A fourth member of the genus, and the only other one to occur in Rhodesia, is *B. tomentosa* which is readily distinguished by its yellow petals, one to three of which are usually blotched with dark reddish purple at the base.

Plate 78

Plate 79

53 Elephantorrhiza elephantina (Burch.) Skeels   *Plate 78*

dwarf elephant-root

Family   Leguminosae; subfamily Mimosoideae

Flowers   October.

Habitat   Grassland or open *Acacia* woodland, on shallow stony soils overlying granite or dolerite; abundant at the foot of the Great Dyke.

Distribution   Extending from the Mtoroshanga area to Salisbury, Marandellas and Juliasdale, and to Gwelo, Que Que, the Matopo hills and Fort Victoria; it is absent from the lowveld. It also occurs in Botswana, Mozambique, Swaziland and the Transvaal.

General   *Elephantorrhiza* is an entirely African genus with only seven species, four of which occur in Rhodesia. The other Rhodesian species are shrubs, but two, *E. goetzei* and *E. burkei*, sometimes reach the proportions of a tree. *E. elephantina* was discovered early last century in South Africa by the celebrated naturalist and traveller William Burchell who described it as an *Acacia* because of its finely bipinnate leaves and its catkin-like flowers. When it was transferred to the new genus specially created for it, the massive rhizomatous root provided an appropriate name, *Elephantorrhiza*. The woody tuberous root is often widely branched and gives rise to what appears to be a colony of separate plants above the ground.

The root of *E. elephantina* has a high tannin content and was used by the early settlers in the Transvaal for the tanning of leather. For the same reason the roots of all four species of *Elephantorrhiza* are used as a cure for diarrhoea and other abdominal disorders.

It is to the subfamily *Mimosoideae* that the large and important genera *Acacia* and *Albizia* belong.

54 Tylosema fassoglensis (Kotschy ex Schweinf.) Torre & Hillcoat

creeping bauhinia   *Plate 79*

Family   Leguminosae; subfamily Caesalpinioideae

Flowers   October to January.

Habitat   Open grassland, glades in woodland; on a wide variety of soils.

Distribution   Throughout Rhodesia, more common at medium to high altitudes on the watershed. From the Sudan southwards to the Transvaal and Swaziland.

General   At one time the genus *Tylosema* was considered to be part of *Bauhinia*, but it has now been separated from *Bauhinia* because of its tendrils and the fact that its pods do not split into two valves. The possession of a huge underground tuber is also a characteristic of the genus. The tuber is very large, reaching up to 3 m or more in length and 15 cm in diameter. From the top of the tuber radiate the prostrate stems which may be up to 6 m in length, but are more usually about 3 m long. The upper petal is small and has two swellings at the base.

T. fassoglensis is very similar to *T. esculenta*, the gemsbok bean of the Transvaal, Kalahari and South West Africa, but it is more robust and has larger, more pubescent leaves which are less deeply divided.

Cattle and game animals browse the pods and leaves of both species. The seeds of *T. esculenta* are said to taste something like cashew nuts when roasted, and the tuber to resemble sweet potatoes. The generic name probably refers to the upper petal, meaning literally 'knob standard'. The specific name *fassoglensis* means 'coming from Fazoghli', the place in the Sudan where it was first collected.

Plate 80

Plate 81

55 Eriosema engleranum Harms — Plate 80

mashona fire bean; blue bush

Family   Leguminosae; subfamily Papilionoideae

Flowers   September to November.

Habitat   *Brachystegia* woodland or open grassland.

Distribution   Very common in Mashonaland, from Macheke to Hartley and north to Concession and Mtoroshanga. It occurs also in Zambia and Malawi, and sparsely in Mozambique.

General   This is a many-stemmed perennial herb which grows from a woody root-stock and reaches a height of one metre or more. The stems normally die off in the winter or are burnt off by early spring veld fires which promote a flush of flowers at ground level. In the absence of fire or heavy frost, flowers are borne on the stems in the axils of the leaves. Mature plants have a characteristic bluish grey appearance.

E. engleranum is dominant over quite large areas and it may sometimes be an indicator of over-grazed veld. Cattle will not eat it green, but apparently relish it in hay when it provides a useful protein supplement to their normal diet. It is surprising that, for a plant so successful in a limited area, it has such a restricted distribution.

E. engleranum is named after Professor Adolph Engler of Berlin-Dahlem who first collected it at Norton and between Hartley and Gadzema. Professor Engler was visiting Rhodesia in September 1905 as one of the delegates to the British Association meeting in Cape Town. The president of the association formally opened the new railway bridge at the Victoria Falls.

56 Eriosema psoraleoides (Lam.) G. Don — Plate 81

canary pea

Family   Leguminosae; subfamily Papilionoideae

Flowers   Mainly from January to April.

Habitat   Stream banks, roadside ditches, edges of cultivation and grassland at vlei margins.

Distribution   Throughout Rhodesia except in the higher parts of the mountains of the eastern border and in the more arid areas of the lowveld. It occurs over the whole of tropical Africa, extending as far south as the Transvaal and Natal, and is also found in the Malagasy Republic.

General   This is an erect bushy perennial herb up to 2 m or more in height. Its conspicuous racemes of canary yellow flowers appear during the second half of the rains. The pea-like flowers are typical of those of the subfamily and the hairy two-seeded oval or oblong pods are typical of the genus. Another characteristic of many species of *Eriosema* is that the leaves and stems have a scattering of small yellow glands.

Eriosema is a pantropical genus with some eighty to ninety species occurring in Africa, of which nineteen are found in Rhodesia. Most of the other eighteen Rhodesian species are smaller than *E. psoraleoides;* all are perennial herbs of grassland or woodland, and some have edible tubers. The seeds of *E. psoraleoides* are sometimes cooked and eaten, and the powdered root is used to treat venereal disease.

The specific name indicates that the plant is reminiscent of *Psoralea*, another genus in the same family. The two Rhodesian species of *Psoralea*, however, show no resemblance to *E. psoraleoides*. The generic name means 'woolly standard', and refers to the woolly or hairy nature of the standard petal.

Plate 82   Plate 83

57 Indigofera dimidiata Vogel ex Walp.

Plate 82

trifoliate indigofera

Family Leguminosae; subfamily Papilionoideae

Flowers December to February.

Habitat In short open montane grassland.

Distribution Inyanga mountains from World's View to the Mtarazi falls, and on the Rhodesian Himalayas. It occurs also on Mount Mulanje in Malawi, in Mozambique, and from the Transvaal along the Drakensberg mountains to Lesotho and the eastern Cape, where it occurs almost at sea level.

General This sprawling herb trails through the grass forming patches of pink when in flower. It is a very distinctive species with its trifoliate leaves and large stipules.

The broken distribution pattern suggests that it may have originally inhabited an area along a range of mountains, now broken, or that colder or wetter geological periods enabled it to live at lower altitudes in what are now tropical areas.

The name *Indigofera* means 'producing indigo' and at one time several species were of importance as a commercial source of indigo for the dye industry. Two of these species, *I. tinctoria* and *I. arrecta*, occur naturally in Rhodesia, but they have never been exploited commercially in this country.

The specific name *dimidiata* means that one half of an organ is so small that the whole organ appears halved; in this instance the organs referred to are the large stipules.

The fruits in *Indigofera* are occasionally one- to two-seeded pods that do not split open (as in *I. nummulariifolia*, a weed of cultivated ground), or flattened pods (as in *I. praticola*), but the vast majority of species have cylindrical two- to many-seeded pods that split open at maturity.

58 Indigofera hilaris Eckl. & Zeyh.

Plate 83

gay indigofera

Family Leguminosae; subfamily Papilionoideae

Flowers September to November.

Habitat Open grassland at medium to high altitudes.

Distribution On the central watershed from Umtali to the Matopo hills, and occurring also from Melsetter to Inyanga and on the Great Dyke. It is generally distributed in suitable habitats from Zaire and Tanzania south to the Transvaal and the eastern Cape.

General This is a deciduous perennial growing new branches each year from a perennial root-stock. It is one of the more showy flowers that comes up after a veld fire. In the Headlands and Marandellas areas it can be seen in extensive patches. It is less spectacular in some seasons than in others, since, if the leaves develop too quickly, the attractive pink flowers are hidden before flowering is finished.

Ecklon and Zeyher must have found this plant equally charming when they first collected it in the Winterberg mountains in the eastern Cape, since they gave it the specific name *hilaris* which means 'gay' or 'cheerful'.

About eighty species of *Indigofera* occur in Rhodesia. These vary greatly in their habit from large shrubs or trees like *I. lyallii* and *I. rhynchocarpa*, to delicate annuals like *I. monantha*.

A character which separates species of *Indigofera* and *Cyamopsis* from other leguminous genera is the possession of hairs with two branches which are often T-shaped: the stalk of the T may be very short and the cross-piece is parallel to the leaf surface.

Plate 84

Plate 85

59 Mucuna coriacea Bak.

Plate 84

subsp. **irritans** (Burtt Davy) Verdc.

buffalo bean

Family   Leguminosae; subfamily Papilionoideae

Flowers   January to May.

Habitat   *Brachystegia* and other types of woodland, river banks and rank bush on hillsides at medium altitudes in subtropical climates.

Distribution   Rather widely distributed in Rhodesia; it occurs on the central watershed but is more common at somewhat lower altitudes, for example at Mazoe, Shamva, Umtali and Zimbabwe. It is not recorded from low altitudes except in the moist eastern part of the country. It is found in Uganda and Zaire and extends southwards on the eastern side of Africa as far as the Transvaal, Swaziland and Mozambique.

General   *M. coriacea* is a climbing or trailing herb reaching about 4 m. It grows from a perennial root-stock from which new stems develop each year. The calyx, wing petals and fruit are covered with copious ginger brown irritant hairs, which outdo any stinging plant in the burning itch they produce if anyone unwisely touches them. When the pods are ripe the whole neighbourhood of the plants seems impregnated with the irritant hairs; even fallen hairs will produce itchy calves and ankles, despite the protection of long trousers.

There are about a hundred species of *Mucuna* occurring throughout the tropics. Two other species are found in Rhodesia: *M. poggei*, a liane which grows in the Pungwe valley and has large pendulous inflorescences of greenish white flowers; and *M. pruriens* which has long trusses of flowers similar in colour to those of *M. coriacea*. The hairs on the pods of both of these species are just as noxious as those of *M. coriacea*. The velvet bean, used in agriculture as a fodder crop and as a green manure, is a variety of *M. pruriens*, and is devoid of any stinging hairs.

60 Mundulea sericea (Willd.) A. Chev.

Plate 85

mundulea

Family   Leguminosae; subfamily Papilionoideae

Flowers   October to December.

Habitat   Mixed woodland and granite outcrops at low to medium altitudes.

Distribution   Throughout Rhodesia below the main watershed. It occurs from West Africa to the Sudan and Somalia, and southwards to South West Africa, the Transvaal, Swaziland and Natal. It is also found in India, Sri Lanka and the Malagasy Republic.

General   *M. sericea* is an attractive bush 2 to 3 m in height, with corky bark and silvery grey foliage. The purple-mauve or lilac sprays of flowers which come out with the commencement of the rains are somewhat reminiscent of *Wisteria*. It can be grown readily, especially if the seed is pre-soaked in warm water. In a mild climate with good care, plants can flower in two to three years.

The bark and seeds are widely used as a fish poison. The active ingredient, rotenone, is also the active principle in *Derris* root which is used in making insecticides.

M. sericea is the only African species. The other thirty species are confined to the Malagasy Republic. The genus is very closely allied to *Tephrosia* and occupies an intermediate position between that genus and *Millettia*. *Tephrosia* is a large and critical genus with some three hundred species, of which about thirty-seven occur in Rhodesia. *Tephrosia vogelii*, like *M. sericea*, is widely used as a fish poison. *Millettia* is a genus of lianes and trees; both the Rhodesian species are trees, the timber of one, *Millettia stuhlmanni*, being known as 'panga panga'.

The origin of the generic name is obscure. The specific name *sericea* means 'silky with long appressed glossy hairs'.

Plate 86

Plate 87

61 Pseudarthria hookeri Wight & Arn.

Plate 86

bug-catcher

Family Leguminosae; subfamily Papilionoideae

Flowers January to March.

Habitat *Brachystegia* and other types of woodland, and rank grassland along watercourses, among rocks and in scrub on mountainsides.

Distribution Widespread in Rhodesia but more common on the eastern mountains and along the central watershed than at lower altitudes. Throughout tropical Africa, extending southwards to Angola, the Transvaal and northern Natal.

General *P. hookeri* is the only species to occur in Rhodesia. It is a perennial up to 2 to 3 metres tall, with stems that die off in the winter. The flower is variously described as pink, reddish purple, blue, rose or white. In Rhodesia the panicles of flowers are mainly pink or reddish purple.

The genus is a small one consisting of four to six species confined to the Old World. It is closely related to the large genus *Desmodium* but differs in that the pod does not break up transversely into several pieces but splits into two valves.

The leaves have slightly curved hairs and therefore catch readily onto other surfaces. Children play with them by sticking them onto their clothes in patterns. The plant is used by Africans to catch bed-bugs: a ring of leafy branches is placed around the sleeping mat; the bugs are caught on the stem and leaves in the morning and can then be burnt.

The generic name means 'false joints', a reference to the pod which looks as if it should develop articulations but does not. The species is named after Sir W. J. Hooker (1785-1865) who became the first Director of the Royal Botanic Gardens at Kew in 1841.

62 Vigna frutescens A. Rich.

Plate 87

trailing fire pea; shrubby vigna

Family Leguminosae; subfamily Papilionoideae

Synonym *Vigna esculenta*

Flowers August to September.

Habitat *Brachystegia* woodland and grassland.

Distribution In Rhodesia it is common on the central watershed from the Matopo hills to Umtali, and occurs also at Fort Victoria and elsewhere. It is widespread in tropical Africa and extends as far south as Angola, Botswana, Mozambique and possibly South Africa.

General *V. frutescens* and its close relative *V. nuda* are amongst the first plants to flower in spring on burnt veld. The latter species can be distinguished by the more erect flower stalk and the richer pink flowers, and the fact that it never develops leaves until flowering has finished. *V. frutescens* has pale mauve flowers, is more intertwined and trailing, and often develops leaves before the flowering period ends. *V. nuda* can also be distinguished by the upwardly-directed pocket on the left-hand side of the keel, a feature which is absent in *V. frutescens*. The stems of *V. frutescens* are normally annual and trailing, and are produced each year from a woody root-stock. However, in fire-protected parts of the Matopo hills it develops into what can only be described as a thick-stemmed liane.

Another showy *Vigna* growing in woodland and flowering at the same time as the other two is *V. pygmaea*, which produces its much smaller flowers well before the leaves.

Besides the three early-flowering species mentioned, there are eleven other species growing wild in Rhodesia. The cultivated cowpea, *V. unguiculata* subsp. *unguiculata*, is widely grown for stock feed. Subspecies *dekindtiana* is wild in Rhodesia.

Vigna is named after Dominic Vigni, a seventeenth century Italian scientist. The specific name means 'shrubby'.

Plate 88 Plate 89

63 Monsonia biflora DC.   *Plate 88*
perennial dysentery-flower

Family Geraniaceae

Flowers September to February.

Habitat Grassland at medium to high altitudes.

Distribution From the Matopo hills to Salisbury and across to Inyanga. It also occurs in Botswana, the northern Cape, South West Africa, Angola and the Transvaal.

General A perennial with annual shoots arising from a woody root-stock, this species grows to about 60 cm tall. The petals are up to 2 cm or more long and are white, sometimes veined or flushed with pink.

Monsonia is a genus of about forty species indigenous to Africa, some of which extend to India and South West Asia.

Three other species occur in Rhodesia: *M. angustifolia* is an erect annual and, in the past, has been much confused with *M. biflora*; *M. senegalensis* is an annual with dark-veined pink flowers which occurs in mopane woodland in the Zambezi valley and in the south and west of Rhodesia; and *M. ovata* is a yellow- or cream-flowered perennial growing in mopane woodland. Four true species of *Geranium*, from which the family takes its name, grow naturally in Rhodesia. The cultivated geraniums, including those which produce geranium oil, belong to the genus *Pelargonium*.

Monsonia was named by Linnaeus after Lady Anne Monson, a great granddaughter of Charles II of England. She spent some of her married life in India and collected plants there and in the Cape with Thunberg and Masson. The specific name, *biflora*, meaning 'two-flowered', is not very apt since the inflorescences are one- to three-flowered.

The common name was applied to this and other species of *Monsonia* by early settlers in the Cape, who used the roots as a cure for dysentery.

64 Pelargonium luridum (Andr.) Sweet   *Plate 89*
variable stork's bill

Family Geraniaceae

Flowers November to February.

Habitat Most common in grassland at medium to high altitudes, but may also occur as low as 1 200 m.

Distribution Occurs from the Matopo hills along the central watershed to Salisbury and across to Inyanga, Umtali and Melsetter. It extends from the eastern Cape northwards to Angola, Zaire and Tanzania.

General The species is extremely variable both in flower colour and in leaf shape. The first basal leaves produced from the perennial root-stock each year are broad, rounded and not much dissected into lobes. Later the leaves become more and more divided. The flower colour, in Rhodesia usually white, cream, yellow, or tinged with pink, may be a deep rose or yellow and red in the Natal Drakensberg, and dark red in southern Mozambique and Angola.

The generic name, *Pelargonium*, is taken from the Greek word for a stork, and refers to the resemblance of the fruit to the head and beak of a stork. The specific name, *luridum*, means 'dingy yellow' and refers to the flower colour.

There are some two hundred and fifty species of *Pelargonium*, most of which occur in South Africa. Only four species, including *P. luridum*, are found in Rhodesia: the bright pink *P. mossambicense* is a plant of grassland and forest margins along the eastern border mountains; *P. apetalum*, a delicate annual with minute flowers, is scattered in a few localities between Inyanga and the Matopos; and *P. graveolens* occurs among rocks on the Chimanimani mountains.

Plate 90

Plate 91

Plate 92

65 Tribulus zeyheri Sond.

large-flowered devil-thorn

Plates 90 and 91

Family Zygophyllaceae

Flowers December to April, after rain.

Habitat On dry open ground, especially in areas which have been over-grazed and trampled, in association with baobabs, mopane, acacias, commiphoras or combretums.

Distribution In Rhodesia *T. zeyheri* is confined to areas fairly close to the Limpopo and Shashi rivers. It extends southwards to the northern Cape and west to South West Africa and Angola.

General This species is very similar to *T. terrestris*, the common devil-thorn which is widely distributed in Rhodesia being most plentiful in the southern lowveld and absent at the highest altitudes. However, *T. zeyheri* differs in that its flowers, being 2,5 to 4 cm across, are more than twice the size of those of *T. terrestris*, and its flower stalks are longer than the subtending leaf. In addition, the spines of the fruit are shorter in *T. zeyheri* than they are in *T. terrestris*. On the fruit of both species there are a number of spines, about four of which are more robust than the rest and are so arranged that at least one will be pointing up when the fruit falls to the ground. They are similar in principle to caltrops (to which the generic name refers), which were iron balls each armed with four sharp prongs so placed that, when thrown on the ground, one prong always projected upwards; caltrops were once used to impede cavalry.

The species is named after Carl Zeyher, the plant collector who was in partnership with C. F. Ecklon, who, from 1840 to 1841, made a lengthy expedition from Cape Town to the Transvaal.

In South Africa, the eating of wilted *T. terrestris* by sheep has been known to cause photosensitivity.

66 Oxalis semiloba Sond.

fish-tail sorrel

Plate 92

Family Oxalidaceae

Flowers December to March.

Habitat On forest margins, in *Brachystegia* woodland and grassland at medium to high altitudes.

Distribution Fairly general in Rhodesia, except at altitudes below about 1 200 m. Widespread in Africa, occurring from the Sudan and Ethiopia south to the Cape.

General This is a perennial herb which has a long vertical rhizome growing from a bulb. Probably because of its extensive range there is considerable variation in leaflet shape and size.

There are an estimated eight hundred species of *Oxalis* occurring throughout the world, of which over two hundred are found in South Africa and six in Rhodesia. Two of the Rhodesian species are troublesome weeds. *O. latifolia* from tropical America somewhat resembles *O. semiloba* but it lacks the vertical rhizome and has leaves which arise directly from the bulbs. It has a very effective method of vegetative reproduction, producing runners from between the leaf bases at the end of which new bulbs are produced. It is extraordinarily difficult to eradicate once it has become established in a garden. The other weed is the yellow-flowered *O. corniculata* which flourishes in lawns, although it is not very unsightly or harmful. Another indigenous yellow-flowered species, *O. radicosa*, is found on river banks, and a further species, *O. obliquifolia*, has solitary pink flowers with yellow centres and is widespread in *Brachystegia* woodland and grassland in Rhodesia.

The generic name *Oxalis* means 'acid', and refers to the sharp taste of the leaves, which contain oxalic acid. The specific name *semiloba* refers to the leaflets which are lobed for about half their length.

Plate 93

Plate 94

Plate 95

67 Sphedamnocarpus pruriens (A.Juss.) Szyszyl. *Plate* 93

canary nettle

Family   Malpighiaceae

Flowers   January to May.

Habitat   Grassland and open woodland, on termite mounds and among rocks.

Distribution   Throughout the medium altitude areas of Rhodesia, ranging from, for example, halfway up the road to the Skyline Pass in Melsetter to the Matopos National Park. It is not found in the lowveld nor in truly montane situations. It occurs from Angola, Zambia, Malawi and Mozambique across to South West Africa, and south to the northern Cape and Natal.

General   This is an erect shrublet or herbaceous to semi-woody scrambler, climbing over low bushes or twining through the grass. Although the plants are perennial the 2 to 3 m long stems normally die back each year. The flowers are about 25 mm across and the leaves vary in shape as well as hairiness.

One rather closely related species, *S. galphimiifolius* from southern Mozambique and Natal, has been recorded in certain parts of Rhodesia.

The family Malpighiaceae, of little economic or horticultural importance, is concentrated in tropical America. The best known species is *Malpighia glabra*, the barbados cherry, the juice of which is used to enrich fruit beverages low in vitamin C. The generic name *Sphedamnocarpus*, meaning 'maple-fruited', refers to the strong resemblance of the winged samaras to those of the genus *Acer* to which the maples and sycamore belong. The specific name means 'stinging' and alludes to the fact that the lower surface of the leaf and the base of the fruit bear hairs that irritate and penetrate the skin.

68 Polygala virgata Thunb. *Plates* 94 and 95

manica pride

Family   Polygalaceae

Flowers   Mainly July to August, but continuing to December; it is usually possible to find some plants in flower at any time of the year.

Habitat   Found in forest margin, rank montane grassland and vegetation along stream banks.

Distribution   Along the mountains of the eastern border from Inyanga to Mount Selinda, reappearing again in the Mazoe district, on Wedza mountain and along streams coming out of the Great Dyke from Darwendale northwards. Extending to Zaire and Tanzania and south to the eastern Cape.

General   This perennial sparsely-branched shrub reaches 3 m in height and makes an attractive show during the latter half of winter. It can be grown easily from seed as a garden ornamental and provides flowers for several months. The cut flowers last well in water. Each flower has two colourful enlarged sepals which, at first, one would take to be petals. The lowest petal of the flower is tipped with a purple crest.

The name *Polygala* means 'much milk', as in Europe there was an old belief that species of *Polygala* or milkworts would increase the milk yield of cows grazing them. The specific name *virgata* means 'twiggy' and in this instance indicates long slender twigs.

Approximately six hundred species of *Polygala* are known throughout the world and of these twenty-five occur in Rhodesia. They range from minute annuals like *P. pygmaea* which is usually not much taller than 6 to 10 cm and is found in dry sand, and *P. africana* which, despite being only 8 to 12 cm high, has quite showy dense racemes of pink flowers, through to *P. virgata* which is the largest species.

Plate 96

Plate 97

69 Gossypium herbaceum L.

Plate 96

var. **africanum** (Watt) Hutch. & Ghose

wild cotton

Family Malvaceae

Flowers December to March is the main flowering period.

Habitat In open mopane, acacia, baobab or other types of mixed woodland at low altitudes, often on basaltic soil.

Distribution Var. *africanum* is found in the Nyamandhlovu area across to Gona-re-Zhou, and in the Sabi valley; it should be looked for in the Zambezi valley in Rhodesia since it was recorded in Mozambique from the area now flooded by Cabora Bassa. It also occurs in Botswana, the Transvaal, Mozambique and Zululand. The typical variety was described from a specimen cultivated in Asia Minor.

General Wild cotton is a perennial bushy shrub usually 1 m in height, but occasionally reaching 2 m or more. In the past it was widely cultivated as the source of cotton, but it has now been replaced by cultivars of *G. hirsutum* which has longer lint hairs. This and *G. barbadense*, the extra long staple Sea Island cotton, are New World species.

Each fruit or boll splits open when ripe revealing a number of seeds with white fuzz. Apart from the many uses of the lint of the cultivated plants, the seeds yield a valuable oil which is used in the manufacture of paint and as a cooking oil; the residue makes a high protein feed for livestock. Cotton is now a major crop in the warmer parts of Rhodesia below about 1 200 m. It is subject to attack by a number of insect pests and consequently requires a rigorous crop-spraying programme. *G. herbaceum*, together with various wild species of *Hibiscus*, and even *Sterculia* and *Adansonia*, are the natural hosts for some of these pests.

Gossypium is an ancient Greek name for the cotton plant.

70 Hibiscus aethiopicus L.

Plate 97

var. **ovatus** Harv.

dwarf yellow hibiscus

Family Malvaceae

Flowers November to March.

Habitat Upland and medium altitude grassland.

Distribution From the Matopo hills and Bulawayo along the watershed to Marandellas and across to Inyanga, Umtali and Melsetter. It occurs from Ethiopia south to the Transvaal and Natal in the eastern half of Africa.

General This is one of the smaller species of *Hibiscus*, being usually less than 30 cm tall. It is a perennial seen to best advantage in areas where the grass has been burnt. The shape of the leaves is variable. The open flowers, which are 6 to 7 cm in diameter, look disproportionately large for the size of the plant. The petals are most often yellow or creamy but may be white when they first open; as they fade they usually turn pinkish.

The species was described from the Cape, not from Ethiopia, as one might expect from the name. In Roman times 'Aethiopia' was a country which extended on both sides of the equator and whose limits were not accurately determined; it certainly did not correspond to modern Ethiopia. In early botanical Latin *aethiopica* therefore simply means 'African'.

There are nearly three hundred species of *Hibiscus* scattered throughout the tropics. The widely grown hedge plant, the chinese hibiscus, *H. rosa-sinensis*, is perhaps the best known member of the genus. A number of its cultivars have variously coloured or double flowers and variegated leaves.

The generic name *Hibiscus* is taken from the Greek word meaning 'marsh mallow'.

Plate 98   Plate 99

71 Hibiscus caesius Garcke   *Plate* 98

dark-eyed hibiscus

Family   Malvaceae

Flowers   January to May.

Habitat   Rocky sites in woodland, especially in *Acacia*, baobab, *Combretum*, and *Commiphora* mixed woodland, and sometimes in riverine vegetation at low altitudes.

Distribution   Throughout the lower lying areas of Rhodesia. It occurs in all the adjacent countries and is widespread in tropical Africa and tropical Asia.

General   This 2 m tall, partly trailing, partly climbing perennial is perhaps the most strikingly attractive of all the yellow-flowered species of *Hibiscus*. The bright yellow flowers with their sharply contrasting dark maroon eyes are widely expanded (about 10 cm in diameter) and borne on thin stalks 15 cm or more in length. The spectacular epicalyx, consisting of seven to nine sharp linear bracts, gives the buds and fruits a spider-like appearance.

The specific name *caesius* is an adjective most often applied to eyes, and can mean 'blue-eyed' or 'grey-eyed'. Here it seems apt to translate it as 'dark-eyed'.

There are about forty-four species of *Hibiscus* recorded from Rhodesia. A large number have similar flowers (yellow with a purple eye) and can only be distinguished by a careful examination of the epicalyx and calyx in conjunction with other characters. *H. physaloides*, however, can be readily recognised even when not in flower since there are always some white chalky concretions on the under surface of the leaf near the petiole.

72 Hibiscus burtt-davyi Dunkley   *Plate* 99

mountain hibiscus

Family   Malvaceae

Flowers   April to July.

Habitat   Among large tumbled boulders on porous acid sands on mountains, either in grass or amongst low shrubs and herbs.

Distribution   Found on the Chimanimani mountains on both the Rhodesian and Mozambique sides, and on the Mozambique side of the Himalaya mountains. It was first described from material collected from Mount Mulanje in southern Malawi.

General   This shrub grows up to 2 m tall in the Chimanimani mountains but becomes a small tree reaching 7 m in height when inhabiting the margins of *Widdringtonia* and *Podocarpus* forest on Mount Mulanje. The stems are covered with rust coloured irritant hairs which are more vicious than those of most members of the genus. The flowers are very distinctive, being usually pale pink or white in colour, and are up to 10 cm in diameter.

The present isolated pockets of distribution point to previous ages having wetter and colder climates and therefore providing species, now only found at high altitudes, with a favourable habitat at lower altitudes.

The species was named after Dr Joseph Burtt Davy (1870-1940), a distinguished British agriculturalist and botanist. He was appointed Agrostologist and Botanist to the Transvaal Department of Agriculture in 1903, and in 1925 became lecturer in Tropical Forest Botany at Oxford.

Plate 100

Plate 101

73 Hibiscus meeusei Exell

Plate 100

small-flowered kenaf

Family Malvaceae

Flowers February to May.

Habitat Roadsides, fallow lands and disturbed areas on a variety of soils.

Distribution Common along the watershed from Umtali to Salisbury and from Zimbabwe to Sinoia. Also recorded from the Victoria Falls and along the eastern border from Inyanga to Chipinga. It is a common weed of cultivation in Zambia, Angola, South West Africa, Transvaal and Swaziland; it also occurs in Malawi and Mozambique.

General This is an annual herb growing to just over a metre tall. It has been confused with *H. mastersianus* as it bears a superficial resemblance to that species; however, the bracts of the epicalyx are always forked in *H. mastersianus*, but are simple in *H. meeusei*.

When in flower the distinction between *H. meeusei* and *H. cannabinus* is very clear, but they are nevertheless very closely related. They differ in that *H. meeusei* is branched from the base, whereas *H. cannabinus* is usually not branched; the stems are pubescent and bristly in *H. meeusei*, whereas in *H. cannabinus* the stems have sparse prickles or, at most, a line of hairs; the flowers of *H. meeusei* are bright yellow with reddish brown centres whereas those of *H. cannabinus* are considerably larger and are greyish sulphur yellow in colour with purple centres.

The bark of some species of *Hibiscus* contains long strong fibres and, in fact, *H. cannabinus* is widely cultivated, under the name kenaf, as an alternative to jute for making sacks. Rosella jelly comes from a similar species, *H. sabdariffa*.

H. meeusei is named after Dr A. D. J. Meeuse, a Dutch born botanist who worked at the National Herbarium, Pretoria, for a few years.

74 Hibiscus dongolensis Del.

Plate 101

dongola hibiscus

Family Malvaceae

Flowers January to May.

Habitat Fertile alluvial soils in hot dry river valleys and open *Acacia* or mopane woodland at low altitudes.

Distribution It is found in most of the low lying parts of Rhodesia, occurring at places such as Wankie, Chirundu, Tuli and Nuanetsi, and is particularly prevalent in the eastern lowveld. It is widespread in tropical and South Africa, extending as far north as the Sudan.

General *Hibiscus dongolensis* is a perennial reaching a height of about 2 m. It is somewhat woody at the base. The showy yellow flowers with their maroon eyes normally appear to be drooping and partly closed; they open fully for only a very brief period in the morning in full sun.

Many of the members of this genus are host to various insect pests which attack cultivated cotton. So far only *H. dongolensis* has been found to harbour the pink bollworm, one of the most serious of the cotton pests. For this reason it is compulsory to destroy all *H. dongolensis* plants occurring close to the lands in the cotton growing areas of Rhodesia.

A closely related species which is sometimes mistaken for *H. dongolensis* is *H. vitifolius*. However, these species can be distinguished by the fact that the latter has a winged and not a subglobose capsule, as does *H. dongolensis*, and that *H. vitifolius* has ten linear bracts below the calyx whereas *H. dongolensis* has five strap-shaped bracts. *H. vitifolius* is a more rounded and compact bush with flowers normally fully expanded; it is the most common species in the Sabi valley, especially near Hot Springs.

The species is named after Dongola, a place on the Nile in the northern Sudan.

Plate 102   Plate 103

75 Pavonia urens Cav.

Plate 102

stinging pavonia

Family Malvaceae

Flowers March to May.

Habitat Found in forest margins and secondary scrub in areas which have over 1 250 mm of rain annually and are therefore potentially able to support evergreen forest.

Distribution In Rhodesia in suitable localities from Inyanga to Mount Selinda, and extending southwards to Natal. It is widely distributed in tropical Africa reaching Guinea in the west and Ethiopia in the east. It also occurs in the Malagasy Republic and in Réunion.

General This is an erect bushy herb, 1 to 3 m tall, well dotted with both soft and sharp hairs, the latter penetrating the skin and causing itching when touched. Over the very wide distribution range there is considerable variation in leaf shape, hair density and flower colour, but there seems little doubt that all these plants are best regarded as a single polymorphic species.

Pavonia is mainly a South American genus; it has over two hundred species, of which only seven occur in Rhodesia. *P. columella* is a smaller forest-edge species with pink or white flowers. *P. burchellii* and *P. senegalensis* are yellow-flowered species of lower rainfall lowveld areas. The remaining three species, which are not so widespread, have an epicalyx which surrounds the bud like a cage.

Pavonia is distinguished from *Hibiscus* in that its fruit consists of five free carpels and ten style branches, rather than a single capsule and five free style branches which characterise the fruit of *Hibiscus*.

The generic name *Pavonia* honours Jose Antonio Pavon M.D. (1745-1844) of Madrid, a traveller in Peru who, with H. Ruiz Lopez, published botanical works on Peru. *Urens* means 'stinging'.

76 Hibiscus rhodanthus Gürke

Plate 103

poppy hibiscus; dwarf red hibiscus

Family Malvaceae

Flowers September to November.

Habitat Open grassland and open *Brachystegia* woodland.

Distribution Gatooma to Salisbury and north to the Zambezi escarpment; it is widespread in Zambia and also occurs in Angola, Tanzania, Malawi and Mozambique.

General In Rhodesia this is normally a deciduous plant, only a few centimetres tall, growing each year from a woody root-stock. The more northerly plants may attain a height of one metre and flower towards the end of the rains, perhaps for a second time.

H. rhodanthus resembles a dwarf flanders poppy and is one of the most striking of all our spring flowers. The vivid red blooms, about 3 cm in diameter, are produced almost directly from the subterranean root-stock. As with most of the spring flowers, the burning of the veld appears to stimulate flowering. This may be due to the heating effect of the fire, but is more likely to be the result of dead grass and other foliage being removed, thus enabling the sun to shine directly on the soil; the consequent warmth would tend to rekindle and hasten growth after dormancy during the cold dry winter.

H. rhodanthus belongs to a natural group of species within *Hibiscus* which was included by Hochreuter in his section *Bombycella*. Members of this group usually have uniformly red flowers with more than five epicalyx bracts, and seeds with a cottony floss. At least twenty closely related Rhodesian species would be included in this group.

The specific name *rhodanthus* means 'red flowered'.

Plate 104   Plate 105

77 Melhania acuminata Mast.

Plate 104

bushy honeycup

Family Sterculiaceae

Flowers January to May.

Habitat Most common in lowveld mopane, *Combretum*, baobab and other types of woodland, but also occurs in *Brachystegia* woodland at higher altitudes.

Distribution Throughout Rhodesia except above 1 500 m, being particularly common in all lowveld areas. It is also found in Botswana, Angola, Zambia, Mozambique and the Transvaal.

General This perennial bushy herb reaches about 60 cm in height and is often found growing under trees. The flowers, which open in the morning and close in the afternoon, are about 2 cm in diameter and are readily distinguished from the closely related *M. forbesii* as the flowers of the former have acuminate epicalyx bracts and styles measuring 7 to 10 mm long, whereas those of the latter have acute epicalyx bracts and styles measuring 1 to 3 mm long. It is therefore quite easy to distinguish the two species when they are seen together. Plants with characters intermediate between the two species occasionally appear; these are quite likely to be hybrids.

A variety, var. *agnosta*, which has scattered dark brown star-shaped hairs has been described from the Transvaal; it has the same distribution as the typical variety.

Besides the two species mentioned, there are four other species of *Melhania* recorded from Rhodesia. The best known of these is *M. randii*, a common flower of the pre-rain flora of the highveld. Like *Hibiscus rhodanthus*, it may flower at ground level or on a stem several centimetres long.

Melhania is named after Mount Melhan in the Yemen where Forskal collected the type species, *M. velutina*. The specific name *acuminata* refers to the shape of the epicalyx bracts which taper abruptly to a point.

78 Wormskioldia longepedunculata Fresen.

Plate 105

rhodesian pimpernel

Family Turneraceae

Flowers November to February.

Habitat Roadsides and fallow lands, *Brachystegia* woodland and grassland on the central watershed, but not in the drier lowveld areas nor much above 1 500 m.

Distribution Widespread in Rhodesia, except in the lowveld below 900 m and at altitudes above 1 500 m. It extends from Tanzania south to Botswana, the Transvaal and Mozambique.

General This perennial reaches 45 cm in height and has annual stems bearing long scattered purple hairs. The flowers are about 3 cm in diameter and open in succession. They provide a bright splash of colour over a long period, although each flower lasts only one day.

The plants are reported to be poisonous to cattle in East Africa, but they are seldom grazed because of their repellent odour. In Rhodesia there has never been any suspicion of toxicity.

W. longepedunculata is the food plant for various butterflies of the genus *Acraea*. These butterflies, all of which have warning colouration and patterns, are distasteful to predators. It is possible that the poisonous properties of their food plants give them their unpleasant taste and immunity.

There are four other species of *Wormskioldia* that occur in Rhodesia: *W. glandilufera*, *W. lobata*, *W. tanacetifolia* and *W. schinzii*. The first three are annuals. *W. schinzii* is closely related to *W. longepedunculata* but has a shorter inflorescence, yellow and not purple hairs on the stem, and leaves which are lobed below the middle.

The genus *Wormskioldia* is named after the Danish botanist M. Wormskiold (1783-1845). The specific name *longepedunculata* means 'with a long flower stalk'.

Plate 106

Plate 107

79 Hypericum roeperanum Schimp. ex A. Rich   *Plate* 106

large-leaved st john's wort

Family Clusiaceae (alternative name: Guttiferae)

Flowers June to November.

Habitat Along streams and at forest edges, generally between 1 500 and 1 800 m above sea level.

Distribution Marandellas, Wedza mountain, Rusape, and at medium altitudes on the mountains of the eastern border. From Ethiopia and the Sudan southwards to Angola, Zambia and the Transvaal.

General Normally a shrub 2 or 3 m tall but occasionally a tree of 4 m or more in height, this species is usually found in rank scrub in sites capable of supporting forest. Its flowers are about 5 cm in diameter and the long flowering period makes it well worth cultivating as a garden ornamental. It is much sought after by bees. The leaves have minute oil glands which, when held up to the light, can be seen as transparent dots and dashes. It is these glands that give the leaves their characteristic and pleasant scent when crushed.

The generic name was derived from a classical Greek name for st john's wort.

Schimper named the plant after a botanical colleague, J. A. C. Roeper (1801-1885).

There are about four hundred species of *Hypericum* occurring mainly in the northern hemisphere; six species are found in Rhodesia.

Certain species of *Hypericum* are toxic to stock, and in South Africa photosensitisation has been induced experimentally in sheep by feeding them on *H. revolutum* and *H. aethiopicum*, both of which occur in Rhodesia.

80 Hypericum revolutum Vahl   *Plate* 107

curry bush

Family Clusiaceae (alternative name: Guttiferae)

Synonyms *H. leucoptychodes; H. lanceolatum*

Flowers June to November.

Habitat In mist belt in mountainous areas at 1 400 to 2 500 m, either forming clumps or extensive patches in grassland, or growing along streams and forest margins.

Distribution Along the mountains of the eastern border of Rhodesia from Inyanga to Melsetter, tending to occur at higher altitudes than *H. roeperanum*, but occasionally found at quite low altitudes in the Melsetter area. It extends from the eastern Cape and Natal through the north-eastern Transvaal to most of the higher mountains of East Africa, reaching Fernando Po and Cameroun mountain in the west and Ethiopia in the north. It also occurs on the mountains of south-western Arabia and in Réunion, the Malagasy Republic and adjacent islands.

General It is normally a dense bush about 2 m high but it can become a tree reaching 6 m or more in height. The aromatic leaves produce a scent likened variously to curry or to roasting coffee. It is one of the plants that produces the characteristic mountain fragrance which makes hiking or trout fishing in the Inyanga National Park so memorable and refreshing.

Like *H. roeperanum*, it can be successfully introduced to gardens, especially in cooler areas which have well drained acid soils rich in organic matter. It can be propagated from cuttings or by seed.

The specific name *revolutum* refers to the revolute leaf margins.

Of the other four species that occur in Rhodesia three, *H. aethiopicum, H. wilmsii,* and *H. peplidifolium*, are herbaceous perennials confined to the eastern border mountains. The last species, *H. lalandii*, is a small variable perennial common in wet areas in grassland at all altitudes throughout the country.

Plate 108   Plate 110

Plate 109   Plate 111

81 Gnidia kraussiana Meissn. *Plates* 108 and 109

yellow-heads

Family Thymelaeaceae

Synonym *Lasiosiphon kraussianus*

Flowers September to October.

Habitat Grassland or the marginal area between woodland and grassland, and along vlei margins.

Distribution Widespread in Rhodesia, being found from Fort Victoria and the Matopo hills north to Miami and Sipolilo, and east from Salisbury along the watershed to the eastern border. It occurs in Natal and the Transvaal northwards to the Sudan and west to Guinea, and so is widespread in tropical and south Africa.

General This is one of the first plants to come into flower after the veld has been burnt. The 30 cm high stems are produced from a perennial woody turnip-shaped root-stock. In the same population, some plants can have hairy leaves and others can be quite without hairs. Thirty to forty bright yellow flowers are borne together in each dense terminal head. The heads are about 3 cm in diameter and are pleasantly scented.

This plant is toxic to stock, but is apparently not often grazed. The root-stock is used as a fish poison in the Chishawasha area. In West Africa the root is used as an arrow poison. Infusions or decoctions of the root are used by African herbalists to treat constipation, food poisoning, ulcers and boils, madness, sore throats, lumbago and snake-bites. Not infrequently, accidental overdoses are given, sometimes with fatal results. The toxic principle has not yet been isolated.

The generic name *Gnidia* is the ancient Greek term for a species of *Daphne*. The specific name was given in honour of the German botanist, Dr Christian Ferdinand Friedrich von Krauss (1812-1890), who made an excellent collection of Natal plants between 1838 and 1840.

82 Combretum platypetalum Welw. ex Laws *Plates* 110 and 111

subsp. **oatesii** (Rolfe) Exell

dwarf red combretum; red wings

Family Combretaceae

Flowers August to October.

Habitat Grassland, especially in marginal areas between woodland and grassland, and open *Brachystegia* woodland.

Distribution Particularly common along the watershed from Bulawayo to Rusape and south to Fort Victoria. In the north it extends to the Zambezi escarpment. It does not occur at low altitudes and is scarce in the eastern part of Rhodesia. It is also found in Zaire, Tanzania, Zambia, Malawi and Mozambique. The typical subspecies occurs in Angola, South West Africa, Zaire and Zambia.

General This is a dwarf shrub with annual prostrate shoots arising from a woody root-stock. In Rhodesia, subsp. *oatesii* is usually under 30 cm tall; however, in the Salisbury area it may occasionally reach more than a metre in height. It is one of the first plants to flower in the spring, especially after a veld fire. The four-winged fruits, which give rise to one of the common names, are typical of the genus, although there are exceptions in that the fruits of some species have five wings and certain coastal species have none.

The green kernel of the fruit has been found to be toxic to human beings and pigs, but the active ingredient has not yet been isolated.

Combretum was the name used by Pliny for a particular climbing shrub, but it is not now possible to be sure what the plant was. The specific name *platypetalum* means 'with broad petals'. Subsp. *oatesii* is named after the naturalist pioneer, Frank Oates (1840-1875), who collected birds and plants in Matabeleland. He died of fever on his way back from the Victoria Falls and his grave is near the Botswana/ Rhodesia border not far west of Plumtree.

Plate 112 Plate 114

Plate 113 Plate 115

83 Combretum paniculatum Vent.   *Plates* 112 and 113

subsp. **paniculatum**

forest flame-creeper

Family Combretaceae

Flowers Mainly August, but recorded as flowering up to November. In Salisbury, under cultivation, it flowers in June.

Habitat Occurring within forest and along forest margins.

Distribution Not common, but widely distributed in forests along the mountains of the eastern border of Rhodesia. It has been noted in the lower Pungwe valley, in Imbeza forest, on Umtali commonage and at Mount Pene and Mount Selinda. It is found throughout tropical Africa from Senegal eastwards to Ethiopia and south to Angola, Rhodesia and Mozambique.

General This forest liane differs from subsp. *microphyllum* in that it bears flowers and leaves simultaneously and has different ecological preferences. Although distinct in appearance, even under cultivation, the flowers of the two plants seem identical, and it would therefore appear that Dr Wickens has made a wise decision in uniting the two taxa under one species.

This subspecies has been grown successfully in the National Botanic Garden in Salisbury. As a screen it rivals *Bougainvillea*; it is initially slow growing but the results are well worth waiting for.

The specific name means 'paniculate' which is the term for an inflorescence in which the axis is divided into branches each bearing several flowers.

There are about two hundred and fifty species of *Combretum* found in the tropics of both the Old and New Worlds. Rhodesia boasts nineteen species, some of which are trees and bushes of considerable ecological importance. Most species have inconspicuous flowers, but are readily recognisable as combretums because of their characteristic four-winged fruits.

84 Combretum paniculatum Vent.   *Plates* 114 and 115

subsp. **microphyllum** (Klotzsch) Wickens

riverine flame-creeper; burning-bush

Family Combretaceae

Flowers August to September.

Habitat River and stream banks and woodland, usually in hotter, lower and drier areas than subsp. *paniculatum*.

Distribution Widespread in Rhodesia at low altitudes, being particularly common in the valleys of the main rivers and their tributaries. It does occur sparingly, however, as far up-river as Lake McIlwaine and near Marandellas. It is found from southern Tanzania south to the Transvaal.

General This creeper favours river banks where it is often found covering trees and bushes. The leaves are shed before flowering so that, when in bloom, it appears as if the whole tree is ablaze — hence the common name, burning-bush. The flowers are usually a lighter shade of red than those of subsp. *paniculatum*, but are otherwise identical, which is why the two taxa have now been placed in the same species.

Like the other subspecies, subsp. *microphyllum* makes a successful garden plant and can be grown as a climber, or pruned and trained as a standard.

The stem of this creeper can be used as a water-vine; a cut section will provide a good drink if one has a panga or machete handy when thirsty. However, the creepers tend to grow near rivers which, even when dry, can often yield water if one digs down for it; it would therefore be a pity to chop down a plant that has taken many years to grow for the sake of two cups of water.

The subspecific name means 'small-leaved'.

Another species, *C. mossambicense*, grows in similar situations to the burning-bush and has attractive white flowers. It is a shrub with supple semi-climbing stems 2 to 3 m or more in height.

Plate 116 Plate 117

85 Dissotis canescens (E. Mey. ex Grah.) Hook.f.   *Plate* 116

marsh dissotis

Family   Melastomataceae

Synonym   *Dissotis incana*

Flowers   December to March.

Habitat   Marshy ground, in the perennially wet part of vleis and along stream banks.

Distribution   Along the eastern border mountains from Chipinga to Inyanga and in vleis along the watershed to Salisbury; also occurring at Bikita, Buhera and Zimbabwe. Widespread in Africa, except in very low rainfall areas, from Nigeria to Ethiopia and southwards via Angola, Zambia and Mozambique to Natal and the eastern Cape.

General   This perennial herb grows to over 1 m in height; the above-ground portion usually dies down in winter. The bright mauve-pink or magenta flowers are 3 to 4 cm in diameter and bloom over several weeks. They would be an attractive addition to the garden but the plants require wet sunny positions and a soil rich in organic matter. They can be propagated by root division or seed and will come into flower in the second season.

The generic name, *Dissotis*, means 'of two kinds', and this is a reference to the stamens: these may be equal, but they are usually markedly unequal, in which case the large stamens differ structurally from the shorter ones. *Dissotis* stamens are of further botanical interest in that the anthers are hinged on the filaments, the tips of the anthers being tucked into special pockets at the base of the flower while still in bud. When the flower opens, the anthers spring free and discharge their pollen through apical pores.

The specific name *canescens* means 'greyish' and refers to the colour of the leaf.

Bantu people in Natal and the Cape are reputed to use this plant to treat dysentery, diarrhoea and hangovers.

86 Dissotis pulchra A. & R. Fernandes   *Plate* 117

chimanimani dissotis

Family   Melastomataceae

Flowers   May to October.

Habitat   Tree lined stream banks and marshy ground on peaty sands overlying quartzites at altitudes over 1 500 m. Sometimes growing with species of *Syzygium* (waterberry).

Distribution   An endemic species confined to the Chimanimani mountains on the Mozambique/Rhodesia border near Melsetter. It has been collected on both sides of the border.

General   In size and appearance this species is intermediate between *D. princeps* and *D. canescens*. It is 1 m tall and is found in dense stands in protected seepage areas.

As with other species of *Dissotis*, the leaves have a series of parallel veins instead of a central midrib. The leaf surface is hairy and rough.

The Chimanimani National Park is rich in Melastomataceae. In addition to *D. pulchra*, both *D. princeps* and *D. canescens* occur on the mountains. The delicate annual *Antherotoma naudinii* is to be found in damp places in montane grassland. *Pseudosbeckia swynnertonii*, a perennial endemic shrub with splendid purple-mauve flowers, grows to 1 m in height and occurs among quartzite rocks — it may be seen even at quite low altitudes. In or near the Haroni-Makurupini forest at the southern foot of the Chimanimanis, but still within the National Park, is to be found *Tristemma mauritianum*, a shrubby herb attaining almost 2 m in height, which has flowers with equal stamens in tight terminal heads. Two further species of *Dissotis*, *D. rotundifolia*, a soft herb rooting at the nodes, and *D. senegambiensis*, an erect perennial with spreading hairs, are also present in this area.

The specific name *pulchra* means 'beautiful'.

Plate 119

Plate 120

Plate 118

87 Dissotis princeps (Bonpl.) Triana   *Plates* 118 and 119

royal dissotis

Family   Melastomataceae

Flowers   May to October.

Habitat   Stream banks and marshy ground at altitudes ranging from 1 500 m to 2 500 m in high rainfall areas.

Distribution   Mainly along the mountains of the eastern border from Chipinga to Inyanga, but also found occasionally in vleis along the watershed. It extends as far as Cameroun, Sudan and Ethiopia in the north and the eastern Transvaal, Swaziland and Natal in the south.

General   A perennial herb or shrub from 1 to 3 m high, this species is very common in eastern Rhodesia. The striking flowers are about 5 cm across and are produced in succession so that a continual splash of colour is provided throughout the winter months. Occasional flowers are sometimes produced in summer. The flowers and stature of the plant are very similar to the widely cultivated South American lasiandra, *Tibouchina semidecandra*. *Tibouchina granulosa*, with its similar but more showy flowers, is a South American tree that has been grown very successfully in the National Botanic Garden, Salisbury. It is covered in flowers and quite spectacular from December to March. The royal dissotis can be grown successfully and often makes a better show than *Tibouchina semidecandra*, but it is not as impressive as *T. granulosa*.

The specific name, *princeps*, means 'distinguished, chief or princely' — hence the common name.

Dissotis is a purely African genus and contains one hundred and forty species in tropical and southern Africa; of these only seven occur in Rhodesia.

88 Erica swynnertonii S. Moore   *Plate* 120

swynnerton's heath

Family   Ericaceae

Flowers   February to May, but often flowers at other times of the year.

Habitat   Damp ground overlying quartzite and granite, along grassy stream banks, above 1 500 m in altitude.

Distribution   Along the higher parts of the eastern border mountains stretching from the Chimanimani mountains in the south to Inyangani in the north. It is also recorded from the Mozambique side of the Chimanimani mountains.

General   This, the most attractive of the Rhodesian heaths, is 25 to 50 cm tall and has a flower which is about twice the size of a match-head. One of the rewards of a day in the mountains is to encounter patches of this dainty pink heath by the headwaters of our trout streams.

Seven other species of *Erica* occur on high ground in the eastern mountains. The hairy *E. johnstoniana* is one of the most common and certainly the most distinctive.

The mountains of the western Cape support the greatest number of heath species, with over one hundred being known from the Cape peninsula alone. A total of about six hundred and five have been recorded from the whole of South Africa. The distribution of the genus extends to Europe and the temperate areas of Asia, where another fourteen species are found.

The generic name *Erica* comes from the Greek word for heath. The species is named after the distinguished naturalist Mr C. F. M. Swynnerton (1877-1938) who farmed at Mount Selinda for a number of years and made the first botanical (and zoological) collections in the Melsetter and Chipinga areas. Many new species were named after him.

Plate 121

Plate 122

89 Chironia purpurascens (E. Mey.) Benth. & Hook.f.   *Plate* 121

subsp. **humilis** (Gilg) Verdoorn

dwarf chironia

Family Gentianaceae

Flowers November to February.

Habitat Damp ground on vlei margins, open grassy stream banks, marshy ground on hillsides, and in roadside ditches.

Distribution From Inyanga to Salisbury along the central watershed, and southwards to Fort Victoria; it occurs also in the Matopo hills. In South Africa it is found over much of the highveld from the Transvaal to the Orange Free State, and it also occurs below the escarpment in the Natal midlands.

General In suitable sites these plants frequently occur in colonies where they form sheets of magenta pink.

On drier ground they grow to 20 cm in height but in more favourable conditions they can reach 50 cm. The flowers are about 2 cm in diameter. This species often grows alongside *C. palustris*, but it may be distinguished from the latter by the fact that it has bluish green leaves and drooping buds, whereas *C. palustris* has erect buds and its leaves lack the bluish tinge.

Chiron was a centaur in Greek mythology concerned with botany and medicine; *purpurascens* means 'purplish' and refers to the flower colour, and *humilis* means 'lowly'.

There are another eight genera belonging to the Gentianaceae that occur naturally in Rhodesia. These include *Sebaea* which contains ten species, most of which have yellow flowers.

90 Chironia palustris Burch.   *Plate* 122

subsp. **transvaalensis** (Gilg) Verdoorn

transvaal chironia

Family Gentianaceae

Flowers October to February.

Habitat Grassy stream banks, vlei margins and damp ground at altitudes of 1 200 to 1 500 m.

Distribution Throughout the higher and wetter parts of Rhodesia from the Matopo hills to Mashonaland and along the watershed to the eastern border. It is also recorded from Victoria Falls, Kyle National Park, Gokwe and Mtoroshanga. It extends into Zambia, Botswana, South West Africa, Swaziland and the Transvaal, with the typical subspecies reaching as far south as the eastern Cape.

General This is an erect perennial with a basal rosette of glaucous obovate leaves. The showy pink flowers, each about 2,5 cm in diameter, have bright yellow anthers which are either straight or slightly twisted. It often occurs in profusion, making a fine show in November before the rains.

It has been proved to be toxic to livestock but they seem to avoid it.

Fifteen species of *Chironia* are known from South Africa, but only four occur in Rhodesia. A particularly attractive species is the trailing *C. gratissima* which inhabits forest margins along the eastern border mountains. The anthers become tightly twisted after flowering, a character which distinguishes it from *C. palustris*. Another Rhodesian species is *C. krebsii* which occurs in the Inyanga area and has clustered flowers, rather long persistent basal leaves and reduced stem leaves. It extends to the Cape and is also recorded from Zambia and Malawi.

The name *palustris* means 'marshy' or 'growing in marshy places'.

Plate 123   Plate 124

Plate 125   Plate 126

91 Adenium obesum (Forsk.) Roem. & Schult.
var. **multiflorum** Klotzsch   *Plates 123, 124 and 125*
sabi star; impala lily
Family   Apocynaceae
Flowers   May to September.
Habitat   Occurring in dry woodland among rocks, on sandy soil or on alluvium at low altitudes where baobabs, mopane and acacias are often dominant.
Distribution   It is found in the Sabi, Limpopo and Zambezi valleys in Rhodesia and extends through the eastern Transvaal and Mozambique into Swaziland and northern Zululand. It is found throughout the drier parts of the eastern side of Africa as far north as the Sudan, Ethiopia and Arabia, and extends also into West Africa.
General   This is a succulent shrub ranging from 30 cm to 3 m in height. It has very swollen lower stems. The leaves, which may or may not be hairy, are clustered at the ends of branches and are normally shed before flowering commences. The flower colour is quite variable and even pure white specimens are known.

In very dry areas it is possible to grow plants from cuttings but elsewhere these will normally rot; propagation from seed is therefore recommended. A sunny dry well drained rockery with alkaline or well limed soil is best.

Forskal recorded the Arabian vernacular name of *Nerium obesum* as Oddaeyn or Aden, and it is from the latter, and not the city, that the generic name is derived. The type specimen came from Mount Melhan in the Yemen. The specific name *obesum* refers to the fat trunk and the varietal name means 'many flowered'.

It is one of the specially protected indigenous plants scheduled under the Parks and Wild Life Act.

92 Strophanthus kombe Oliv.   *Plate 126*
zambezi tail flower
Family   Apocynaceae
Flowers   October to November.
Habitat   Dry mixed lowveld woodland, often on rocky ground.
Distribution   In Rhodesia in the Limpopo, Lundi, Sabi and Zambezi valleys and elsewhere at low altitudes. It occurs from Tanzania south to the north-eastern Transvaal and Mozambique.
General   This is a rambling shrub with flexible arched branches growing to about 3 m in height; however, it is sometimes a strong climber reaching 10 m in height. The mature leaves are large, hairy and crinkly above. The stems are rough and hairy. The plant is leafless throughout the dry season and it is then that the extraordinary seed pods are particularly noticeable. The fruit consists of two smooth narrow pods each 20 to 40 cm long joined at the base to form, as it were, one long pod with tips pointing in opposite directions. These paired fruits are characteristic of members of the Apocynaceae. The pods contain seeds with long silky parachutes for wind dispersal.

The corolla of the flower has twisted tails, and it is this feature which has given rise to the generic name which means 'twisted flower'. The specific name *kombe* is from an African vernacular name for the plant.

The seeds of this species are recognised in the British Pharmacopoeia as the official source of strophanthin. Livingstone and Kirk first reported on the use of *S. kombe* as one of the ingredients in the making of an arrow poison. Strophanthin is a powerful cardiac poison but, when injected in small quantities intravenously, it raises the blood pressure and acts as a diuretic. Strophanthin is still in demand and collection of seeds in the wild in Malawi is still a profitable, though minor, industry. The Batonga people of the Zambezi valley use the leaves to poultice festering wounds.

Plate 127   Plate 128

93 Ceropegia nilotica Kotschy *Plate* 127

white-banded ceropegia

Family Asclepiadaceae

Flowers December to February.

Habitat Woodland of various kinds, for example mopane, *Acacia*, and *Brachystegia*, usually at altitudes below 1 200 m.

Distribution Fairly widely distributed in Rhodesia, occurring in Matabeleland and the Zambezi valley, and recorded also from Mrewa and Zimbabwe. It extends northwards to the Sudan and south to South West Africa, the Transvaal and Natal.

General This slender creeper grows to 2 or 3 m, and produces flowers about 5 cm long. The flowers vary over its extensive range so that it now includes several former species; this broad view of *C. nilotica* was taken by H. Huber when he monographed the genus in 1957.

In the one hundred and sixty species of *Ceropegia* there is considerable diversity of flower shape. The corolla lobes, which arch over the mouth of the tube and are usually joined at their tips, are formed into some exceedingly bizarre shapes; they may resemble an old-fashioned bird-cage or a parasol, or be extended in a long slender column widened into a knob at the top. Their strange beauty is enhanced by remarkable colour combinations which make them difficult to see in amongst a mass of vegetation, but very obvious once they have been discovered. In tropical Africa a common habitat for ceropegias is in the neighbourhood of waterfalls, but they are found in a wide variety of situations. A character that most ceropegias share is a climbing stem growing from a single tuber or bunch of fleshy roots.

The generic name means 'wax fountain', an allusion to the form of the flower. The specific name *nilotica* means 'from the Nile' and refers to the area in which the type specimen was collected.

94 Glossostelma carsonii (N.E.Br.) Bullock *Plate* 128

maroon milkweed

Family Asclepiadaceae

Flowers December to January.

Habitat *Brachystegia* woodland, often on rocky hillsides.

Distribution Found from Umtali and Inyanga along the central watershed to Gwelo and Selukwe, and north to Mazoe and Karoi. It extends westwards to Angola and north to Zaire and Tanzania by way of Zambia and Malawi.

General The annual deciduous stems are about 45 cm in height and arise from a large underground tuber. The flowers are about 2 cm in diameter.

Members of the Asclepiadaceae usually produce paired seed pods which contain numerous seeds, each with a parachute-like tuft of long silky hairs. The pods ripen and burst, releasing the seeds which can then be carried away by the slightest breeze.

Most members of the Asclepiadaceae have opposite leaves and a milky sap. The stamens and style are greatly modified in most Asclepiadaceous genera and not readily recognisable for what they are. Further, the pollen is often united into two waxy masses joined by a short connective, a feature which is present also in the orchids.

The name *Glossostelma* refers to the tongue-like lobes of the corona. The species is named after Alexander Carson (1850-1896) who, after being appointed engineer for the first steamer to operate on Lake Tanganyika, subsequently stayed on at the Fwambo Mission station near Mbala in Zambia. Between 1888 and 1894 he collected four hundred and fifty plant specimens which he sent to Kew.

Plate 129

Plate 130   Plate 131

95 Astripomoea malvacea (Klotzsch) Meeuse   *Plate* 129

common star-creeper

Family Convolvulaceae

Flowers Mainly September to January.

Habitat *Brachystegia* woodland and grassland at medium to high altitudes, and edges of cultivation and woodland on alluvial soils at low altitudes.

Distribution Widely distributed in Rhodesia except at high altitudes. Found also from Cameroun to Ethiopia and south to South West Africa and Natal.

General *Astripomoea* was, for many years, called *Astrochlaena;* however, a new name had to be created when it was realised that the latter was already in use as the name for a fossil fern. *Astripomoea* means 'star Ipomoea', a reference to the star-shaped hairs which cover the leaves and stems of species of *Astripomoea;* the possession of these hairs is a diagnostic feature of the genus within the Convolvulaceae.

A. *malvacea* is a perennial with deciduous annual trailing stems arising from a woody root-stock. It is so variable that the extremes of variation have several times been described as separate species. The flowers are among the first to appear before the rains. They last only one day, opening in the morning and fading before nightfall.

The specific name *malvacea* is derived from the plant's similarity to a species of *Malva*.

The powdered roots are prescribed by Shona herbalists for a number of ailments.

A second species of *Astripomoea* is recorded from Rhodesia: *A. lachnosperma*, an erect annual with purple-centred white flowers which grows in low altitude woodland.

96 Ipomoea kituiensis Vatke   *Plates* 130 and 131

kitui morning-glory

Family Convolvulaceae

Flowers March to May.

Habitat In granite sand and on granite outcrops in low altitude woodland.

Distribution Zambezi and Sabi valleys and elsewhere in Rhodesia at low altitudes. It is found also from Malawi north to Ethiopia.

General This species may be erect and form a bush 2 metres tall; however, it may twine where support is available, in which case it can develop into a robust creeper up to 5 metres in height. The corolla is variously described as being white, shell pink or pale mauve, and in Kenya it may even be yellow with a purple eye. The fruiting capsules contain large ovoid seeds covered with long golden hairs.

I. kituiensis is occasionally seen in cultivation, and a number of other species of *Ipomoea* are commonly grown in gardens. *I. batatas* the sweet potato, is cultivated for its large edible, somewhat fibrous, roots. *I. alba* is a fast growing annual or perennial climber with sweetly scented white flowers which have a tube up to 12 cm long and a salver-shaped limb up to 16 cm in diameter; the buds can actually be observed opening just as the light fades. *I. intrapilosa*, a handsome white-flowered tree-ipomoea, is fairly common in Salisbury gardens. Another common but less spectacular garden shrub is *I. fistulosa*.

The name *Ipomoea* is derived from the Greek and means 'similar to bindweed'. The lesser bindweed found in Europe is known as *Convolvulus arvensis*, but it could easily pass as an *Ipomoea;* the difference between the genera lies in the shape of the stigma. The specific name means 'from Kitui', a village about one hundred and fifty kilometres east of Nairobi.

Plate 132

Plate 133

97 Ipomoea ommaneyi Rendle

Plate 132

ox potato

Family Convolvulaceae

Flowers December to February.

Habitat *Brachystegia* and other types of woodland and marginal grassland.

Distribution On the central watershed from Umtali to the Matopo hills. It extends through the Transvaal and Botswana to the northern Cape.

General This robust prostrate creeper forms mats 2 to 3 m in diameter. The leaves are covered above and below with silky silvery white hairs and these, together with the very rich magenta flowers, give it a strong resemblance to *I. pellita*. The latter, however, differs in that it has linear bracteoles and sepals and is endemic to the eastern Transvaal and Natal. Other species which appear quite closely related to *I. ommaneyi* are *I. atherstonei* and *Turbina oblongata*. The fact that these two species, although placed in separate genera, look so very much alike seems to be an argument for including *Turbina* as part of *Ipomoea*.

In certain homelands in South Africa, the dry crushed root-stock of *I. ommaneyi* is mixed with sour milk and eaten; its leaves are greatly relished by cattle, as are those of *I. batatas*, the sweet potato. *I. aquatica*, which grows in lowveld pans, is reputed to be a good spinach.

The species is named after Captain H. T. Ommaney who botanised in the Transvaal during the Anglo-Boer war; the common name is a translation of the Afrikaans apellation.

The genus contains at least five hundred species and most of these occur in the tropics.

98 Ipomoea shirambensis Bak.

Plate 133

zambezi morning-glory

Family Convolvulaceae

Flowers September to October.

Habitat *Acacia/Commiphora* woodland and lowveld thicket.

Distribution Zambezi and Sabi river valleys and along their tributaries. It occurs from Tanzania southwards to Mozambique, the Transvaal and Botswana.

General This deciduous perennial climbing shrub may be seen near the Victoria Falls and around Birchenough bridge when the trees are dry and leafless before the rains. The striking pale mauve flowers clustered in the otherwise drab and lifeless bush cannot fail to catch the eye of even the most impatient motorist. The heart-shaped leaves appear during the rains after the flowers.

Sir John Kirk first collected this plant at Chiramba (Shiramba) on the Zambezi river during his Zambezi Expedition with Dr Livingstone between 1858 and 1863 — hence the specific name *shirambensis*.

There are some fifty species of *Ipomoea* that occur naturally in Rhodesia. They range from annual weeds with small white or pale mauve flowers, for example *I. eriocarpa*, *I. plebeia* and *I. sinensis*, to woody climbers, such as *I. verbascoidea* and *I. shupangensis*. Some are perennials that flower before the rains, for example *I. blepharophylla* and *I. welwitschii*, while others, like *I. aquatica* and *I. rubens* grow in wet situations.

Plate 134   Plate 136

Plate 135   Plate 137

99 Merremia kentrocaulos (Steud. ex C.B.Cl.) Rendle *Plate 134*

rough-stemmed merremia

Family Convolvulaceae

Flowers December to April.

Habitat *Colophospermum* or *Acacia* woodland in hot dry areas at low altitudes.

Distribution Sabi, Limpopo and Zambezi river valleys and their tributaries. It extends over the whole of tropical Africa, from Sudan and Ethiopia south to Angola, Botswana, the Transvaal and Mozambique, and also occurs in India.

General This woody twiner climbs up to 10 m when suitable trees are available; otherwise it forms extensive prostrate mats which may be seen on roadsides in the southern lowveld. The pale lemon yellow flowers with their dark purple eyes are 6 to 8 cm in diameter and are particularly noticeable in the morning; by the afternoon they have faded and closed. There is a considerable degree of variation in the pattern of dissection of the leaves.

The genus is named after Blas Merrem who was Professor of Economics at Marburg, Germany, very early in the nineteenth century. The specific name *kentrocaulos* refers to the small purple tubercles found on the stems.

Merremia superficially resembles *Ipomoea* but has smooth pollen and white or yellow flowers. In Rhodesia there are only two yellow-flowered species of *Ipomoea*: *I. obscura* and *I. tuberculata*.

Merremia is a genus consisting of about eighty species, of which seven occur in Rhodesia. The most widespread species is *M. tridentata* which has narrow hastate leaves with several teeth on the basal lobes. It is a common woodland and roadside species.

100 Turbina holubii (Bak.) Meeuse *Plates 135, 136 and 137*

rock turbina

Family Convolvulaceae

Flowers January to April.

Habitat *Brachystegia*, *Colophospermum*, *Acacia* or mixed woodland, often on rocky slopes on a variety of soils.

Distribution Widely distributed in Rhodesia at medium to low altitudes. Occurs also in Botswana, South West Africa, Zambia, Malawi, Mozambique and the Transvaal.

General This shrubby perennial has many slender half-climbing branches, usually reaching between 1 and 2 m in height. The leaves, which are shed in winter, have silvery hairs that add to the beauty of the plant. It is well worth a place in the garden and will flower in the second year if grown from seed.

Turbina differs from *Ipomoea* in that the capsule remains indehiscent even when ripe, whereas in *Ipomoea* the capsule splits into four or more valves to release the seeds. Species of *Turbina* are very similar in general appearance to *Ipomoea*, but they tend to be more woody, being subshrubs, shrubs or woody climbers, rather than twining or prostrate herbs.

T. holubii is named after Emil Holub, an Austrian doctor who practised in Kimberley from 1872 and made several collecting expeditions to the north.

There are three other turbinas that occur in Rhodesia: *T. oblongata* which has already been mentioned in connection with its similarity to *Ipomoea ommaneyi*; *T. stenosiphon*, a tall climbing shrub which has a white salver-shaped corolla about 5 cm in diameter with a slender tube up to 13 cm long; and *T. shirensis*, a robust climber reaching 15 m in length, festooning trees with its silky hairy leaves and its white funnel-shaped flowers which are up to 2 cm long.

Plate 138

Plate 139

Plate 140

101 Lantana trifolia L.   *Plate* 138

ternate lantana

Family Verbenaceae

Flowers December to March.

Habitat *Brachystegia* woodland and riverine vegetation.

Distribution In Rhodesia apparently so far only recorded from high rainfall areas in the eastern part of the country, being common from Inyanga to Mount Selinda. Widespread in tropical America and possibly introduced into Africa where it is widespread in tropical and South Africa; it is also found in Asia.

General There are many American plants that have become naturalised as weeds, but rarely have introduced species been able to compete and become part of the natural African vegetation; if *L. trifolia* is an introduction, then it is one of the few that has been successful in this respect. Introduced plants will usually only hold their own in disturbed areas although some are so aggressive that they begin to affect the ecological balance. Strangely enough some of the other species that have proved to be adaptable also belong to the Verbenaceae; for example, both *Verbena bonariensis* and *Duranta repens* are introductions from America. *Lantana camara*, cherry pie, was introduced as an ornamental and as a hedge; under certain conditions, perhaps due to frost or wilting, it may cause photo-sensitisation and liver damage to cattle who eat it. It is spread mainly by birds, and is so aggressive in certain areas that it has become a real menace.

It is not at all clear whether *L. trifolia* was introduced or is a natural world-wide plant; indeed in Kenya it was described as a new species, *L. mearnsii*. There are at least three indigenous species of *Lantana* in Rhodesia.

The name *Lantana* was originally applied to the European genus *Viburnum*, and the specific name, *trifolia*, means 'with leaves in threes'.

102 Trichodesma physaloides (Fenzl) A.DC.   *Plates* 139 and 140

bells of st mary's

Family Boraginaceae

Flowers July to November.

Habitat Grassland in transition zone between woodland and vlei.

Distribution Throughout Rhodesia, except in the hot dry low-veld. Extends northwards to Zaire and the Sudan and southwards to the Transvaal.

General This is one of the first plants to flower in the spring, and it will even flower at the height of the winter or dry season, if stimulated by early veld fires. Like many spring plants, it flowers more vigorously if the vegetation has been burnt. It has been suggested that veld burning stimulates flowering because, by stripping the soil of cover, it allows the sun to heat up the earth more quickly.

It is a perennial species with a large root-stock from which annual stems up to 50 cm in height arise, dying down each winter. The flowers normally appear before the leaves and range in colour from white through very pale lilac to a very light blue. The corollas are often tipped with brown. It does not last as a cut flower, but would be worth growing in a garden; the seeds should be sown in situ.

The root-stock is widely used medicinally by African herbalists to treat many ailments including skin diseases, back-ache and impotence.

A second species of *Trichodesma* which occurs in Rhodesia is *T. zeylanicum*, an annual weed found at low to medium altitudes.

The generic name *Trichodesma* means 'bound by hairs' and refers to the hairs which unite the stamens. The specific name *physaloides* means 'like *Physalis*' (the cape gooseberry), the point of resemblance being the enlarged calyx of the fruits.

Plate 141

Plate 142

103 Leonotis dysophylla Benth.

Plate 141

wedge-leaved leonotis

Family Lamiaceae (alternative name: Labiatae)

Synonym *Leonotis randii*

Flowers February to April.

Habitat Grassland and *Acacia* or *Brachystegia* woodland on sandy soil.

Distribution Found in Matabeleland but there is one record of it growing at Ruwa near Salisbury; it occurs also in South West Africa, Botswana and in all provinces of South Africa.

General This is an erect perennial herb with a number of stems per plant. The flower buds are grouped in 4 to 6 green balls on the upper portion of each stem and are some 5 cm across; from them arise a succession of velvety orange flowers. The three other Rhodesian species share this feature.

L. dysophylla and *L. mollissima*, soft-leaved herbs from the eastern border mountains and Wedza mountain, are the most attractive of the Rhodesian species of *Leonotis*. However, neither matches the splendour of the South African and Zambian *L. leonurus*. The flowers of all species produce a quantity of clear sweet nectar, appreciated by sunbirds and school children alike. Old stems with their series of unusual round balls are most attractive in flower arrangements.

Species of *Leonotis* are used by African herbalists for a variety of medicinal purposes throughout tropical and South Africa. The name 'wild dagga' is applied to various South African species because of a supposed narcotic effect when smoked, but it is apparently innocuous and does not resemble *Cannabis* at all.

L. nepetifolia, the most widespread species in Rhodesia and indeed in Africa, is a tall weedy annual.

The generic name *Leonotis* means 'lion's ear', a reference to the hairy corolla. The specific name *dysophylla* means 'stunted leaf'.

104 Scutellaria paucifolia Bak.

Plate 142

purple banner

Family Lamiaceae (alternative name: Labiatae)

Flowers August to November.

Habitat Grassland at margins of vleis or in open veld.

Distribution Along the central watershed from Salisbury south to Selukwe, east to Inyanga and Melsetter, and north to the rim of the Zambezi escarpment. To the north it reaches as far as Guinea, Sierra Leone, Nigeria and the Sudan.

General This perennial herb has a woody root-stock which, each year in early spring, sends up a number of stems, about 30 cm tall. The dark rich purple blossoms are amongst the first to appear in the new season. As with many other species which bloom before the rains, flower production seems to be initiated and invigorated by the burning of the veld.

The generic name *Scutellaria* means 'dish' or 'little shield' and refers to the shape of the upper lip of the two-lobed calyx which covers the basal part of the flower. The specific name means 'few leaved', an allusion, presumably, to the fact that, when flowering, very few leaves are developed.

Scutellaria contains some three hundred species. They occur in all parts of the world, except South Africa, but most are from the temperate northern hemisphere. Only one species is found in Rhodesia.

Members of the Lamiaceae are generally aromatic; this family includes many of the well known herbs such as mint, thyme, sage, marjoram, basil and rosemary.

Plate 143

Plate 144

105 Pycnostachys urticifolia Hook.   *Plate* 143

large hedgehog-flower

Family   Lamiaceae (alternative name: Labiatae)

Flowers   April to June.

Habitat   Rocky ground in *Brachystegia* and other types of woodland, and rocky stream banks, or grassland in the transition zone between vlei and woodland.

Distribution   From the Matopo hills and Zimbabwe north to Salisbury and along the central watershed to Inyanga, Umtali and Chipinga. It extends as far south as the north-eastern Transvaal, and extends north through Malawi and Mozambique to Tanzania.

General   Hedgehog-flower bushes average almost 2 m in height and are perennial herbs or shrubs with a preference for damp situations. The flowers are a startling shade of blue but unfortunately only a few are produced at one time. The sharp pointed calyx lobes become stiff and spine-like in fruit, a feature which has given rise to the common name.

Selection and breeding would be worthwhile in an attempt to increase the flower size and number of flowers produced at a time. They can be propagated from cuttings or from seed and, if sown early enough, will flower at the end of the same season.

Pycnostachys means 'dense flower-spike'. The specific name means 'with leaves like *Urtica*', the latter being the genus which contains the nettles; this must be a reference to the leaf shape only as the leaves of the hedgehog-flower have no stinging hairs.

Pycnostachys has a total of thirty-seven species confined to tropical and southern Africa and the Malagasy Republic. Three other species occur in Rhodesia in addition to the two included here; these are *P. dewildemaniana* and *P. orthodonta* which are annuals found in moist habitats, and *P. reticulata*, a perennial inhabiting vleis on the eastern border mountains.

106 Pycnostachys stuhlmannii Gürke   *Plate* 144

vlei hedgehog-flower

Family   Lamiaceae (alternative name: Labiatae)

Flowers   March to May.

Habitat   Vleis and damp grassy stream banks, most often on granite, at altitudes ranging between 1 350 and 1 650 m.

Distribution   Inyanga to Umtali and westwards along the watershed extending north to Sipolilo and Bindura and south to Lalapanzi, Zimbabwe and Buhera. It occurs from Zaire and Uganda southwards to Rhodesia.

General   This is an erect perennial reaching 1,5 m in height. It is locally common in suitable situations, especially where a stream meanders through a vlei. This species would be a most desirable garden subject and, if given a damp sunny position, could be cultivated quite easily. Each plant has a large number of flower spikes and these produce a succession of striking clear blue flowers over a long period until all the buds are exhausted or it is eventually cut back by frost.

P. stuhlmannii differs from *P. urticifolia* in that the dried calyx is not stiff and prickly, and the leaves are narrower and have finely toothed margins.

The species is named after Franz Stuhlmann (1863-1928).

Plate 145

Plate 146

107 Aptosimum lineare Marl. & Engl.   *Plate* 145

veld violets

Family Scrophulariaceae

Flowers December to March.

Habitat At low altitudes in mopane and other types of woodland, on granite sands, loams or basalt soils where ground cover is sparse or non-existent.

Distribution Common in Matabeleland near Bulawayo and in the Matopo hills, extending into the lowveld at Beitbridge and found throughout the south eastern lowveld to the Sabi valley, its most northern point of distribution in Rhodesia being Hot Springs. It occurs also in southern Angola, South West Africa, Botswana, the northern Cape and the Transvaal.

General This is a perennial usually reaching between 10 and 20 cm in height. Some specimens are more compact and cushion-like than others. These plants, with their dark blue or violet flowers, 10 to 12 mm in diameter, are characteristic of over-grazed lowveld woodland.

Other species of *Aptosimum*, notably *A. depressum* of the Karoo, form compact mats and have therefore come to be known as carpet flowers.

Another species, *A. decumbens*, which flowers towards the end of the rains, occurs in the extreme north-west of Rhodesia.

The name veld violets refers only to the colour of the flower, as *Aptosimum* is neither related to any of the true violets, nor does it closely resemble them in flower shape. The generic name means 'not deciduous', and refers to the fruits which remain on the plants long after the seed has been shed. The specific name *lineare* refers to the long narrow leaf.

108 Solanum panduriforme Drege ex Dunal   *Plate* 146

bitter apple

Family Solanaceae

Flowers November to January.

Habitat More frequent at medium to low altitudes and found mainly on roadsides, fallow lands and farm yards, and any other type of disturbed ground. It is common on large termite mounds.

Distribution Widespread throughout Rhodesia. It occurs from Uganda and Kenya southwards to the Cape.

General This is an erect branched shrub reaching up to 1 m in height. The stems and leaves are sometimes armed with prickles, but this is a very variable character in *Solanum*. It is regarded by some as being indistinguishable from, or at most no more than a subspecies of, *S. incanum*, a larger and more spiny plant with larger fruits (30 to 40 cm) and a coarser covering of stellate hairs. However, in Rhodesia it would seem appropriate to regard *S. panduriforme* as a separate species, with *S. delagoense* being a synonym of it.

The yellow fruits, and particularly the unripe ones, are poisonous. The fruits, roots and stems are extensively used by Africans for treating a wide variety of ailments including rheumatism, coughs, toothache, piles, ringworm, snake-bites, ear-ache, headaches, and syphilis.

Solanum is a huge genus containing over a thousand species, of which about seven occur in Rhodesia.

Many economic plants belong to the Solanaceae; these include potato, tomato, tobacco, chilli, cape gooseberry, egg-plant and several others.

Solanum was the Latin name for woody nightshade (*S. dulcamara*). The specific name *panduriforme* means 'fiddle-shaped' and refers to the shape of the leaf.

Plate 147

Plate 148

109 Craterostigma plantagineum Hochst.   *Plate* 147

blue carpet

Family Scrōphulariaceae

Flowers October to May.

Habitat Glades in mopane woodland on alkaline soils, or in shallow soil on granite outcrops.

Distribution Widely distributed throughout Rhodesia wherever suitable habitats occur. Extends from the Transvaal to the Sudan, Ethiopia and Arabia.

General After the first good rains, these plants carpet pans and soil pockets. Each plant is only about 5 cm high and has small flat rosettes of leaves and blue flowers. This species has an unusual method of overcoming drought in that at any stage of development it is able to become dormant, the leaves and flower stems withering and drying up. It can remain in this condition for up to several months if undisturbed, and then, within twenty-four to forty-eight hours of warm soaking rain, the apparently lifeless crumpled grey leaves and flower buds become green again and growth continues.

A second species, *C. nanum*, which has mauve and white flowers and smaller narrower leaves, occurs along the eastern border mountains and westwards along the central watershed as far as Marandellas. Another species, *C. monroi*, grows in soil pockets on granite kopjes, and flowers when these fill with rain water.

The generic name *Craterostigma* means 'stout stigma', implying that a conspicuous stigma is a feature of this genus, The specific name *plantagineum* means 'like a plantain' (*Plantago* sp.) and refers to the appearance of the leaves.

110 Cycnium adonense E. Mey. ex Benth.   *Plate* 148

white ink-plant

Family Scrophulariaceae

Flowers November to December.

Habitat *Brachystegia*, *Acacia* and other types of woodland or grass-land above 1 100 m.

Distribution From Bulawayo along the watershed to Gwelo, Enkeldoorn, and Salisbury and then east to Umtali and along the eastern border mountains from Inyanga to Chipinga. It also occurs at Fort Victoria. It is widespread throughout tropical and southern Africa from the Sudan and Ethiopia south to the eastern Cape.

General Like some other genera in the Scrophulariaceae, such as *Striga* and *Alectra*, *C. adonense* is a partial parasite and attaches itself to the roots of other plants from which it draws moisture and nutrients. It is a perennial herb with prostrate branches bearing opposite toothed leaves that are better developed than is often the case with a partial parasite. The pure white flowers are about 6 cm in diameter and are sweetly scented. The leaves and flowers turn bluish black when handled, hence the common name, ink-plant.

The genus *Cycnium* has about forty species, all confined to tropical and southern Africa; only *C. adonense* occurs in Rhodesia. It is rather closely related to *Rhamphicarpa*, the main point of difference being that the capsule is fleshy and indehiscent in *Cycnium*, and beaked and dehiscent in *Rhamphicarpa*.

The generic name *Cycnium* is evidently derived from the Greek word for swan, possibly in allusion to the white flowers. The specific name *adonense* means 'from Addo', the latter being the area in the eastern Cape where the plant was first collected.

Plate 149

Plate 150

111 Graderia scabra (L.f.) Benth.

Plate 149

pink ground-bells

Family Scrophulariaceae

Flowers Mainly between September and December.

Habitat Montane grassland among rocks at altitudes of over 1 800 m.

Distribution Along the eastern border mountains from Inyangani to the Chimanimanis, occurring at such places as the Mtarazi falls, Stapleford, Musapa mountain and Tarka forest reserve. It extends northwards as far as the Nyika plateau in Malawi, and southwards via the Transvaal Drakensberg, Swaziland and Natal to the eastern Cape, where it even occurs on the coast.

General This low growing perennial, 15 to 20 cm tall, occurs in short open grassland. It flowers most profusely after a fire, the flowers being about 30 mm long and varying from pink to pinkish mauve.

There are only three species in the genus of which one occurs in Socotra and one in South Africa.

G. scabra was first described by Carl von Linné as being a member of *Gerardia*, a genus named after the English botanist John Gerard (1545-1612) and which is now regarded as being confined to America. George Bentham transferred *G. scabra* to a new genus which he named *Graderia*, an anagram of *Gerardia*. The specific name *scabra* means 'rough' or 'scabrid' and refers to the hairy leaves and stem.

The family Scrophulariaceae takes its name from the northern hemisphere genus *Scrophularia*, the species of which were used to treat scrofula, a lymphatic disorder.

112 Rhamphicarpa tubulosa (L.f.) Benth.

Plate 150

vlei ink-plant

Family Scrophulariaceae

Flowers December to February.

Habitat Damp grassland and wet vleis.

Distribution Widespread in Rhodesia in higher rainfall areas, but unaccountably rare or absent in the eastern districts. It is widely distributed in Africa from Nigeria to Ethiopia and south to the eastern Cape, and occurs also in the Malagasy Republic.

General This species is apparently a partial parasite of grasses or other plants. The erect stems arise each year from a short perennial rhizome. The leaves are somewhat reduced, an advantage in withstanding flooded conditions during heavy rains; the thin flexible stems also offer little resistance to storm water.

The flowers and stems readily bruise and turn black so it cannot be used as a cut flower, nor could the plants be cultivated except in a marsh garden. However, they are very decorative in the wild, their white, mauve or pale pink flowers somewhat resembling petunias.

Rhamphicarpa is a genus of some thirty species, four of which occur in Rhodesia. *R. heuglinii* is a close relative of *R. tubulosa* but grows in somewhat drier conditions and has white flowers and trailing stems; it is especially common in Matabeleland. The other two species, *R. fistulosa* and *R. filicalyx*, are erect branched annuals with narrow divided leaves, and are widespread in marshy places such as seepage zones on granite outcrops; they both have small white flowers with narrow corolla tubes.

The generic name *Rhamphicarpa* means 'beaked fruit', and the specific name *tubulosa* refers to the tubular shape of the flower.

Plate 151

Plate 152

113 Sopubia mannii Skan — Plate 151
common sopubia

Family Scrophulariaceae

Flowers January to March.

Habitat Vlei and damp montane grassland.

Distribution Widely distributed in Rhodesia, occurring at Gokwe, Wankie, Matopos, Selukwe, Zimbabwe, Mtao and Marandellas, and on the mountains of the eastern border from Inyanga to Melsetter. It occurs from the Ivory Coast east to Uganda and Tanzania and south to Natal and the eastern Cape.

General This is an erect perennial up to 40 cm or more in height growing from a woody root-stock. The conspicuous flowers are mauve-pink in colour.

There are about forty species in the genus, occurring from tropical and South Africa and the Malagasy Republic to tropical Asia; one species has been recorded from Queensland, Australia.

Six species are found in Rhodesia: *S. parviflora*, the only annual species, is known from Karoi; *S. simplex* has ribbed stems and small leaves more or less appressed to the stems and is well distributed at higher altitudes; *S. welwitschii* occurs at Umtali and has flowers with woolly calyces and no pedicels; *S. angolensis* has pedicellate flowers with hairy calyces and is widely distributed, being recorded from Banket, Matopos, Marandellas and Salisbury; *S. ramosa* is a robust perennial which has flowers with relatively short pedicels and leaves with a distinct midrib.

The generic name *Sopubia* is derived from 'sopubi swa', the Indian vernacular name for the type species. The Rhodesian species was named after Gustav Mann who was the British representative in the Gulf of Guinea from 1859 to 1863. He made some excellent botanical collections in the area and climbed Cameroun mountain with Richard Burton, the explorer, in 1861. It was there that he first collected *S. mannii*.

114 Sutera carvalhoi (Engl.) Skan — Plate 152
manica sutera

Family Scrophulariaceae

Flowers July to October.

Habitat Rocky hillsides, forest margins and montane grassland from 1 200 m to 2 000 m.

Distribution On the eastern border mountains from Inyanga to the Chimanimanis, occurring also on Gorongosa mountain in Mozambique.

General This is a rounded bushy perennial up to 1,2 m in height with slightly viscid leaves. It bears numerous flowers, each about 15 mm in diameter, which are white with orange-brown throats.

There are about one hundred and thirty species of *Sutera*, most of which are South African, but a few species are recorded from tropical Africa, and one species occurs in the Canary Islands. In Rhodesia eight species have been recorded, of which *S. carvalhoi* is the largest in both flower size and stature. Another showy species is *S. fodina* which has white or yellowish flowers, almost as large as those of *S. carvalhoi*; it is found only on the serpentine soils of the Great Dyke. *S. burkeana*, which is widespread in Rhodesia, has flowers similar to those of *S. carvalhoi*, but much smaller. A yellow dye is extracted from the brown flowers of a closely related species, *S. atropurpurea*; in South Africa this dye is used as a substitute for saffron, a substance normally obtained from the stigma of *Crocus sativus*. *S. floribunda* is most common in the mountains of the eastern border and has mauve flowers with yellow throats. *S. micrantha* is a weedy species with yellow flowers.

The genus *Sutera* is named after the Swiss botanist J. R. Suter (1766-1827). The species was named after Dr M. R. P. de Carvalho (1848-1909) who first collected this species on Gorongosa mountain.

Plate 153

Plate 154

Plate 155

115 Striga elegans Benth.   *Plate* 153

elegant witchweed

Family Scrophulariaceae

Flowers November to March.

Habitat It occurs in a wide variety of situations from montane grassland to *Brachystegia* and *Baikiaea plurijuga* (rhodesian teak) woodland.

Distribution Common along the eastern border mountains but occurring sporadically elsewhere. It is recorded from Chizarira, Gokwe, Insiza, Gwampa, Beatrice, Fort Victoria and Buhwa mountain.

General *S. elegans* is about 20 cm tall and has somewhat reduced leaves. It is a partial parasite of grasses, its roots penetrating those of the host plant.

There are about forty species of *Striga* found in Africa, Asia and Australia, with six species occurring in Rhodesia. Three of these are sometimes weeds of crops. The maize witchweed, *S. asiatica*, and the giant maize witchweed, *S. forbesii*, are common parasites of veld grasses, but when opportunity arises both will parasitise maize. The tobacco witchweed, *S. gesnerioides*, is normally a parasite of wild legumes, but in a limited area one strain sometimes parasitises tobacco. The seeds of witchweeds are as fine as dust and a single plant of *S. asiatica* can produce up to one million seeds which can be carried as far as ten kilometres by the wind.

The generic name *Striga* probably refers to the fact that some of the species are covered with strigae, or stiff bristles. The specific name *elegans* refers to the handsome flowers.

116 Selago thyrsoidea Bak.   *Plates* 154 and 155

var. **austrorhodesiaca** Brenan

inyanga selago

Family Selaginaceae

Flowers March to July.

Habitat Montane grassland among rocks in the mist belt at about 2 000 m. It has become very common on roadsides and embankments.

Distribution In Rhodesia this variety is confined to the Inyanga Downs. The typical variety occurs on Mount Mulanje in southern Malawi, and a further variety, var. *nyikensis*, is described from the Nyika plateau in northern Malawi and northern Zambia.

General This is a bushy perennial, rather like a heath in appearance, reaching up to 40 cm in height and with a spread of as much as 60 cm or more. The plants have short woody stems and numerous branches covered with fine, slightly aromatic, heath-like leaves. When in full bloom they are an unforgettable sight. The individual mauve-blue flowers are very small, but the crowded heads more than make up for this.

Most of the one hundred and fifty species of *Selago* occur in South Africa. Apart from *S. thyrsoidea*, one other species, *S. welwitschii*, is found in Rhodesia; it occurs mainly on Kalahari Sand, but is found also on sandveld from Rusape to Gutu and Mtao.

The genus *Walafrida* is also a member of the Selaginaceae; it differs from *Selago* in that its calyx is three-lobed instead of being five-lobed. Two species of *Walafrida* occur in the eastern border mountains and two are found elsewhere in Rhodesia.

The generic name *Selago* was used by Pliny to denote one of the club-mosses, *Lycopodium selago*. The similarity between *Selago* and a club-moss lies in the small size of the leaves and the leaf arrangement. The specific name means 'like a thyrse', the term for a compact inflorescence which is thick in the middle and tapers at each end. The varietal name means 'from Southern Rhodesia'.

Plate 156   Plate 157

Plate 158   Plate 159

117 Podranea brycei (N.E. Br.) Sprague   *Plates* 156 and 157

zimbabwe creeper

Family Bignoniaceae

Flowers April to September.

Habitat Forest margins, bases of granite kopjes and riverine vegetation from 500 to 1 500 m.

Distribution Mainly from Inyanga to Mount Selinda in suitable situations. It also occurs at Marandellas, in the upper Mazoe valley, at Zimbabwe, Buhwa mountain and the Lundi river.

General Fred Eyles used the name zimbabwe creeper for specimens he collected at Mazoe as early as 1906. This liane climbs over bushes and trees to a height of 10 to 15 m and provides a beautiful display during the winter months. It has become a very popular garden subject and is easily grown from seed or cuttings. The flower colour varies in intensity from plant to plant, and cuttings are therefore the most satisfactory method of propagation if one wishes to select specimens that have the most deeply coloured flowers.

The only other species in the genus, *P. ricasoliana*, the port st john's creeper, is found in a limited area on the Transkei coast.

The generic name *Podranea* is an anagram of *Pandorea*, an Australian genus in which the port st john's creeper was at one time included. The species was named after the Rt Hon. James Bryce, who sent a specimen of *Podranea* from Mashonaland to Kew in 1896.

The Bignoniaceae also include many cultivated trees and climbers that originated in America, for example the jacaranda *Jacaranda mimosifolia*, the yellow elder *Tecoma stans*, and the golden shower *Pyrostegia venusta*. The few African members of the family include such well known trees as the nandi flame *Spathodea campanulata* and the sausage-tree *Kigelia africana*.

118 Rhigozum zambesiacum Bak.   *Plates* 158 and 159

zambezi gold

Family Bignoniaceae

Flowers September to November.

Habitat Often on shallow stony soils, or on alluvium or alkaline soils, in mopane and *Commiphora* or baobab woodland at about 500 m.

Distribution Found in the Zambezi, Sabi, Limpopo, Nuanetsi and Lundi river valleys, and scattered over the lowveld in suitable locations. It occurs also in Mozambique, the Transvaal and Natal.

General This is a nondescript shrub or bush, about 2 m tall, which, for the greater part of the year, would not merit a second glance. However, with the first heavy rains, it is transformed into a plant of almost unbelievable beauty with every branch and twig becoming laden with brilliant yellow flowers, each 3 cm in diameter. Flowering lasts for only about a week, after which winged seeds are produced in shortly beaked elliptic capsules approximately 5,5 cm long by 1,5 cm wide.

Another species, *R. brevispinosum*, is found in Rhodesia, but is confined to the south and west of the country; it may be distinguished by its simple leaves, as *R. zambesiacum* has small pinnate leaves.

Vast areas of the northern Cape and South West Africa are occupied by *R. trichotomum*, and *R. obovatum* is prevalent in parts of the Karoo. Both species provide valuable browse for sheep and goats.

The meaning of the generic name *Rhigozum* is somewhat obscure; it may mean 'stark and rigid', alluding to the bareness of the shrub before it comes into flower. The specific name means 'from the Zambezi', a reference to the fact that it was originally collected by Kirk near the Zambezi river at Tete.

Plate 160

Plate 161

119 Ceratotheca triloba (Bernh.) Hook.f.   *Plate* 160

african foxglove

Family Pedaliaceae

Flowers November to May.

Habitat On shallow soils among boulders, on granite outcrops, or in *Brachystegia* woodland, but probably most common on roadsides and in other disturbed situations.

Distribution Widespread in Rhodesia except at the highest altitudes and in the driest part of the lowveld. It extends into Botswana, Angola, Zambia, and Mozambique, and southwards through the Transvaal and Natal to the eastern Cape.

General This erect annual herb, about 1,5 m in height, is very common along roadsides where it makes a very attractive display from Christmas onwards. The plant has a pungent disagreeable odour, especially when the leaves are crushed. Although reminiscent of the foxglove of Europe, the african foxglove belongs to the sesame family and not to the Scrophulariaceae.

There are about nine species of *Ceratotheca*, all of which occur in tropical and South Africa. Apart from *C. triloba*, only one other species, *C. sesamoides*, is to be found in Rhodesia; it has very much smaller purplish pink flowers and is not usually more than 60 cm in height.

Besides the four genera of the Pedaliaceae that are included in this book, the following three also occur in Rhodesia in the hot dry river valleys of the lowveld: *Sesamothamnus*, which has only one Rhodesian species, *S. lugardii*, an unusual small tree shaped like a miniature baobab; *Pterodiscus*, whose species have short succulent stems and showy orange or purple flowers; and *Holubia*, whose sole species has greenish yellow flowers.

The generic name *Ceratotheca* means 'horned capsule', the possession of which serves to distinguish this genus from *Sesamum*. The specific name refers to the three-lobed leaves.

120 Sesamum alatum Thonn.   *Plate* 161

wing-seeded sesame

Family Pedaliaceae

Flowers December to March.

Habitat On sandy alluvium along lowveld rivers, on Kalahari Sand in *Baikiaea plurijuga* (rhodesian teak) woodland, and sometimes a weed of cultivation.

Distribution Common in Matabeleland and along the Sabi river, but found also in most of the lower lying areas of Rhodesia. It has a very wide distribution in Africa, from Senegal and Mali across to Sudan and Ethiopia and thence down to South West Africa, Botswana and Mozambique.

General This is an erect annual herb up to 1 m tall which is often found as a weed on disturbed sandy soils and dry river banks. The flowers are about 35 mm long. The leaves differ in size and shape, ranging from the upper leaves which are long and narrow, to the lower ones which are divided almost to the base into 3 to 5 narrow lobes.

There are thirty species of *Sesamum* of which six occur in Rhodesia: *S. angustifolium* which has no lobed leaves; *S. alatum* which has seeds winged at both ends and unlobed upper leaves; *S. capense* which has seeds winged laterally and at one end, and divided upper leaves; *S. triphyllum* which has seeds with only a minute wing or appendage; and *S. angolense* which has hairy leaves. The sesame of commerce (*S. indicum*) is grown on a small scale by farmers in the Tribal Trust Lands; the oil obtained from the seeds is used in cooking.

The generic name *Sesamum* was used by Hippocrates in ancient Greece. The specific name means 'winged' and refers to the seeds.

Plate 162

Plate 163

121 Dicerocaryum zanguebarium (Lour.) Merr.   *Plate* 162

stud thorn

Family Pedaliaceae

Synonym *Pretrea zanguebarium*

Flowers December to April.

Habitat Roadsides and bare ground or old lands on granite sands, and sometimes in amongst sparse short grass.

Distribution Throughout most of Rhodesia, except the very dry lowveld and the higher mountain areas. Extends south to Natal, Swaziland, the Transvaal, the northern Cape, Botswana and South West Africa, and north to Angola, Zambia, Malawi, Mozambique, Tanzania and Kenya.

General This is a prostrate plant which has trailing annual stems arising from a perennial root-stock. It covers about a square metre or more, and thus helps prevent excessive erosion on the bare soil on which it grows. The flowers are up to 35 mm long. The fruit is oval in outline and bears a pair of sharply pointed spines on the upper side. These spines penetrate the feet of animals or become attached to shoes or tyres, enabling the seeds to be effectively dispersed. The plant produces a copious slimy mucilage when immersed in water; in the past it was used as a substitute for soap, and is still favoured by Africans as a lubricant for childbirth.

The generic name is derived from Greek, and means 'two-horned nut'; *zanguebarium* is the latinised form of Zanzibar, although the plant was actually collected on that part of the African mainland known as the Zanzibar Coast. There is only this one species in the genus.

122 Harpagophytum procumbens DC.   *Plate* 163

grapple plant

Family Pedaliaceae

Flowers December to February.

Habitat On bare soil in hot dry areas at low altitudes. Usually in *Acacia*, *Commiphora* and *Combretum* woodland at altitudes ranging from 500 to 1 000 m.

Distribution In the Limpopo drainage system in Rhodesia, from Nuanetsi to Beitbridge and Antelope Mine. Also in the northern and western Transvaal, Botswana and South West Africa, and in the south-western corner of Zambia.

General This plant is probably known to every student of botany and biology as being a classic example of seed dispersal by animals. It is a prostrate mat-forming perennial with trailing annual stems covering one square metre or more. The flowers are about 5 cm long and from them develop the fruits for which the grapple plant is renowned. These vary considerably, with the most fearsome forms occurring from the western Transvaal to South West Africa. Each dry mature fruit has a number of slightly flexible slender woody arms, 6 to 8 cm long, tipped at the ends with several strong recurved teeth. When an animal puts its foot on one of these fruits, the teeth hook into the skin, enabling the seed to be transported some distance before it is dislodged. The Rhodesian plants, especially those in the east, tend to have fruit with much shorter arms.

The generic name, derived from Greek, means 'grapple' or 'hook plant'. The specific name *procumbens* means 'prostrate' or 'lying down'.

Plate 164

Plate 165

123 Streptocarpus michelmorei B. L. Burtt

Plate 164

chipinga streptocarpus

Family Gesneriaceae

Flowers January to April.

Habitat Damp shaded banks, mossy rocks and sheltered cliff faces; often in forest at altitudes ranging from 1 000 to 1 500 m.

Distribution From the Umtali to the Chipinga districts, including the Chimanimani mountains on both sides of the border with Mozambique, and thence east to the Serra Mocuta; it has also been recorded from the banks of a tributary of the Busi river, near the road from Espungabera to Gogoi.

Plants from the Vipya plateau in Malawi may be the same species, or possibly a closely related but undescribed entity.

General Like many other species in this interesting genus, the chipinga streptocarpus has only one leaf. This normally attains a length of 20 to 30 cm, but near the Rusitu Mission in the Ngorima Tribal Trust Land in Melsetter district, enormous leaves of over 60 cm in length occur. The plant takes about two to four years to reach flowering size. In dry winters the lower half of the leaf dies off, but growth is resumed in summer. The flowers also are quite variable. Typically they should have a moderately straight tube with a deep violet bar around the lower rim of the throat, with some yellow behind this. Some flowers have corolla tubes which are almost S-shaped, with either a violet or white V pointing up into the throat.

Many spectacular *Streptocarpus* hybrids and cultivars, which are popular greenhouse subjects throughout the world, have been developed.

The generic name *Streptocarpus* means 'twisted seed pod'. The species is named after A. P. G. Michelmore, an entomologist who collected it on the Inyamadze river near Mount Selinda in 1938.

124 Streptocarpus eylesii S. Moore

Plate 165

common rhodesian streptocarpus

Family Gesneriaceae

Flowers November to April.

Habitat Apparently always on granite, either in damp sites under large boulders or in the open amongst rocks and grass in *Brachystegia spiciformis* (msasa) woodland.

Distribution In Rhodesia it occurs from the Matopo hills to Selukwe, at Chinamora north of Salisbury, Rusape, World's View at Inyanga, Umtali and the Vumba mountains. It also occurs on Gorongosa mountain in Mozambique and reaches Malawi, northern Zambia and southern Tanzania.

General This is the most widespread streptocarpus in Rhodesia. It is a one-leafed species which, like *S. michelmorei*, normally flowers only once. The plant takes about two to four years to reach flowering size. There is some variation in flower colour according to the different localities in which it is found; however, the most common shade is pale blue tinged with violet or mauve.

Eight of the one hundred and thirty-two species of *Streptocarpus* occur in Rhodesia. Two of them, *S. pumilus* from Salisbury to Rusape and *S. hirticapsa* from the Chimanimanis, are extremely small. The lovely magenta-veined *S. cyanandrus* from World's View, Inyanga, has two small leaves. The white-flowered, narrow-leaved *S. umtaliensis* is from the Vumba. The pale-flowered *S. solenanthus* also has only a single leaf and comes from Inyanga and Umtali. *S. grandis* subsp. *septentrionalis* comes from Melsetter and the Chimanimanis.

S. eylesii was first collected by Fred Eyles (1864-1937) in the Matopo hills in November 1902. Eyles farmed at Mazoe and made a large collection of plants between 1901 and 1937. In 1916 he published the first checklist of Rhodesian plants, entitled *A Record of Plants collected in Southern Rhodesia*.

Plate 166

Plate 167

125 **Barleria hirta** Oberm.

Plate 166

hairy barleria

Family Acanthaceae

Flowers February to April.

Habitat Rocky outcrops in the higher rainfall areas at altitudes of about 1 600 m.

Distribution Along the eastern border mountains, especially in the Melsetter area, and along the central watershed to Rusape and Chilimanzi, occurring also at Bikita and Buhera. Its range extends northwards to Tanzania and it is also found in Mozambique.

General A shrubby perennial about 50 cm tall growing from a woody root-stock, this is one of several superficially rather similar species with mauve-blue flowers to be found in various parts of Rhodesia. However, its narrow leaves and lack of spines help to distinguish it from those which it most resembles. Some of the other blue-flowered species include *B. kirkii* which is common in the Sabi and Zambezi valleys; *B. spinulosa* which has wider and more spiny bracts; *B. aromatica*, a bush 1 m tall with sticky aromatic leaves which is found on the serpentine soils of the Great Dyke and at Umtali; *B. crassa*, a spiny species with small thick leaves which is common on granite kopjes over much of the central watershed, particularly from Rusape to Salisbury; *B. eylesii* which is a very spiny species recorded from the Matopo hills; and *B. lugardii* which is a Kalahari Sand species.

Linnaeus named the genus *Barleria* after J. Barelier, a French botanist who died in 1673. The specific name *hirta* means 'hairy'.

126 **Barleria randii** S. Moore

Plate 167

matopos apricot barleria

Family Acanthaceae

Flowers December to January.

Habitat *Combretum/Acacia* woodland on shallow brown loams overlying schist on ridges, or on anthills; it is tolerant of highly mineralised soils.

Distribution Matopos, Bulawayo and Nkai.

General This 30 to 40 cm tall spiny perennial with its handsome foliage and apricot yellow flowers would be an attractive addition to a rock garden.

It belongs to the section *Prionitis* which includes those species with spines and orange or yellow flowers. The most common species in this section found in Rhodesia is *B. senensis* (*B. eenii*) which is widespread in the Zambezi, Sabi, Lundi and Limpopo valleys. Other Rhodesian species in this yellow-flowered section are *B. crossandriformis* recorded from the Nuanetsi river, *B. rhodesiaca* recorded from Wankie and the Zambezi valley, and *B. ameliae*.

Some species of *Barleria* are white-flowered: *B. albostellata*, a common bush in the Matopo hills, has large flowers and is completely covered in white stellate hairs, and *B. elegans* is a riverine species of the south-eastern lowveld.

Most of the estimated two hundred and fifty species in the genus are from tropical Africa; a few, however, occur in the American and Asian tropics.

B. randii is named after Dr R. F. Rand (1856-1937), an English doctor who came to Salisbury in 1890 as the official doctor for the Pioneer Column. He was one of the earliest plant collectors in Rhodesia, and his specimens are still preserved in the British Museum (Natural History) in London.

Plate 168

Plate 169

127 Crossandra mucronata Lindau

sabi crossandra

Family Acanthaceae

Flowers November to March.

Habitat Mopane and *Acacia* woodland on sand and alluvium at altitudes ranging from 200 to 500 m.

Distribution Found in the lower Sabi valley from Birchenough bridge down to the Sabi/Lundi river junction, and probably present in Mozambique. It also occurs in Tanzania and northwards to Uganda and Somalia.

General This attractive plant is a perennial averaging 30 cm in height. It grows in leaf litter beneath mopane trees, in full sun on bare ground beside roads, or in over-grazed areas on deep fertile alkaline alluvial soils.

The compact size of this plant and its handsome flowers, which are produced over an extended period, make it a most desirable subject for rock gardens in drier areas, and indeed some species have been grown in green-houses in Europe.

There are about fifty species of *Crossandra* occurring in tropical Africa, the Malagasy Republic and Arabia. Three other species occur in Rhodesia: *C. greenstockii*, which has toothed but not spinescent bracts, occurs in the Inyanga district; *C. spinescens*, which has bracts with spinescent teeth, and yellow or red flowers, is found mainly in the Zambezi valley, but is also known from the Odzi river; and *C. puberula*, which has papery bracts almost without hairs and with red flowers, occurs mainly at low altitudes in the east and south-east of Rhodesia.

The generic name *Crossandra* means 'fringed anthers', an allusion to the normally hairy anthers. The specific name *mucronata* refers to the bracts which end in a short stiff point.

Plate 168

128 Justicia elegantula S. Moore

elegant justicia; spring posy

Family Acanthaceae

Flowers August to October.

Habitat Grassland or *Brachystegia/Julbernardia* woodland at altitudes ranging from 1 000 to 1 600 m.

Distribution Most common along the watershed from Rusape to Salisbury but widespread elsewhere. It is found throughout Zambia and Malawi.

General This is one of the characteristic and attractive plants of burnt veld in early spring. The pretty flowers are small but densely clustered, and are mauve-pink in colour with contrasting purple stripes. At flowering this perennial is a dwarf cushion usually only a few centimetres high. It can, however, attain a height of 60 cm in summer when it becomes a straggly weed with scattered flowers which are scarcely noticeable among the grasses and other plants. A number of species of *Justicia* are recorded from Rhodesia, but this is by far the most attractive, and well deserves its specific name.

There are altogether about three hundred species in the genus, most of which occur in the tropics and subtropics. However, about fourteen species are known from Rhodesia; these include two yellow-flowered species, *J. flava*, an annual of low altitudes, and *J. odora*, a small shrub of mopane woodland found in the south and west of the country. Two other justicias which are fairly often encountered are *J. matammensis*, an annual weed with small white flowers, and *J. nyassana*, a purple-flowered species of forest edges.

The genus is named after a noted Scots gardener, James Justice, F.R.S.

Plate 169

Plate 170

Plate 171

129 Thunbergia alata Boj. ex Sims

Plate 170

black-eyed susan

Family Acanthaceae

Flowers December to July.

Habitat Rank herbage on roadsides in the more humid areas near forest margins.

Distribution In Rhodesia, black-eyed susan is confined to the mountains along the Mozambique border, being most common around Melsetter and on the Vumba mountains near Umtali. It extends from Natal up to Kenya and Ethiopia and across to Sierra Leone, and is also recorded from Mauritius.

General This is a prostrate creeper or climber growing over low bushes. The delicate stems, arising from a perennial root-stock, may reach a length of 2 to 3 m; they produce a succession of flowers, each about 3 cm in diameter. It is readily grown from seed.

There are some two hundred species of *Thunbergia*, all of which occur in the tropics of the Old World. Of these about nine species are to be found in Rhodesia. *T. alata* is the only one with a dark eye. Of the others, five are entirely yellow, cream or white, and three are blue: *T. huillensis*, an erect species found in *Brachystegia* woodland, has yellow or creamy white flowers; *T. reticulata*, a twining species with small creamy white or yellow flowers occurs mainly on Kalahari Sand; *T. dregeana* is a trailing species with pure white flowers; *T. subalata* is a twining species, rather like *T. alata* but lacking the eye; and *T. petersiana* is an erect white-flowered forest species.

The specific name *alata* means 'winged', and refers to the winged petioles of the mature leaves.

130 Thunbergia lancifolia T. Anders.

Plate 171

early blue thunbergia

Family Acanthaceae

Flowers August to November.

Habitat Open grassland or along the edge of *Brachystegia* woodland.

Distribution Most common along the watershed from Rusape to Salisbury, but frequent throughout Mashonaland and along the foothills of the eastern border. Widespread in Zambia and throughout much of tropical Africa as far north as Ethiopia.

General This is a perennial reaching about 60 cm in height with erect annual stems arising from a woody root-stock. It is one of the first plants to appear in spring after the vegetation has been burnt, and is locally very common. The flowers vary from pale to dark blue, sometimes tinged with violet, and have a rich yellow throat; they are about 5 cm in diameter, but are unfortunately not suited for cutting as they only last one day and fall soon after picking. It would be best grown from seed as it does not transplant satisfactorily. There are two other blue-flowered thunbergias in Rhodesia, both of which occur in the eastern districts: *T. natalensis*, an erect species with broad leaves and light blue flowers, which is found on the edge of montane forests; and *T. crispa*, a woody twining bush with beautiful dark blue flowers.

The genus is named after the Swedish botanist and explorer, Karl Peter Thunberg (1743-1828), who collected in the Cape from 1772 to 1775 and wrote a fascinating four-volume account of his travels.

The specific name *lancifolia* means 'with leaves shaped like a spear-head'.

Plate 172   Plate 173

131 Ruspolia hypocrateriformis (Vahl) Milne-Redh.   *Plate 172*
var. **australis** Milne-Redh.

red mock-plumbago

Family Acanthaccac

Flowers February to May.

Habitat Found at the edges of kloof forests, in *Androstachys* and *Brachystegia glaucescens* woodland, or in mixed bush on rocky slopes.

Distribution From the Sabi valley escarpment near Rupisi Hot Springs in Chipinga district to Gona-re-Zhou and Mateke hills, and along the Lundi escarpment to the Nyoni hills with an apparently isolated occurrence in the Matopo hills at Maleme dam. In South Africa it occurs on the Soutpansberg and across to Punda Maria. The typical variety is found in West Africa from Angola to Senegal.

General This shrubby plant is very similar in shape and appearance to the well known blue plumbago, *Plumbago auriculata*. Its magnificent sprays of red flowers (each bloom being about 2 cm in diameter) make it readily visible from afar. This species would be highly suitable for gardens in the warmer frost-free areas, either as a free-. standing shrub or as a hedge plant.

All four species of *Ruspolia* are African, of which three occur in Rhodesia. *R. decurrens* has inflorescences up to 30 cm in length and calyces with glandular hairs, and *R. seticalyx* has shorter inflorescences, up to 15 cm long, and calyces that are hairy but which lack glandular hairs. Both species have handsome red flowers and favour hot dry areas such as the Zambezi valley.

The genus is named after Count Eugenio Ruspoli who led a collecting expedition between 1892 and 1893 to Somalia and Ethiopia. The specific name *hypocrateriformis* means 'salver-shaped', a reference to the flower which has a long narrow tube expanding into a short open trumpet or shallow bowl. The varietal name *australis* means 'southern'.

132 Leptactina benguelensis (Welw. ex Benth. & Hook f.)
R. Good   *Plate 173*

ivory carpet

Family Rubiaceae

Flowers October to November.

Habitat *Brachystegia* woodland on granite sandveld at altitudes ranging from about 1 200 m to 1 600 m.

Distribution Common in Mashonaland around Salisbury, but found almost wherever *Brachystegia* woodland occurs in Rhodesia; it is absent from the west and the southern lowveld. It extends through Zambia, where it is almost universal, to Angola.

General In Rhodesia this species forms a dense green carpet. Unlike some plants in which flowering is initiated by fires, the flowering of *L. benguelensis* is stimulated by a soaking rain, although the actual blooms only appear after one or two further showers have fallen. The result is that all the flowers open at once and make a striking show. The star-shaped ivory white flowers are sweetly scented and are reminiscent of gardenias, to which they are fairly closely related. The elongated orange fruits are edible.

The generic name, derived from Greek, means 'thin rays', a reference to the radial corolla lobes of some species. The specific name means 'from Benguela', the latter being the place in Angola where this plant was first collected. Twenty-five species are known in the genus, all of which are shrubs of tropical or South Africa. Only two species occur in Rhodesia, *L. benguelensis*, described above, and *L. delagoensis*, a shrub of 2 m or more in height which occurs in the eastern and south-eastern lowveld and also in Mozambique.

Plate 174

Plate 175

133 Mussaenda arcuata Lam. ex Poir.   *Plate 174*

forest star

Family Rubiaceae

Flowers January to April.

Habitat Forest margins and riverine forest from 750 m to 1 500 m.

Distribution Mainly on the eastern border mountains from Inyanga to Chipinga, but also along streams and in relict forest patches in northern Mashonaland and the Binga district. It extends throughout tropical Africa up to Ethiopia and across to Nigeria and Sierra Leone. Found also in Mauritius and the Malagasy Republic.

General This shrub has scrambling or arching branches 2 to 5 m long. The clusters of bi-coloured starry golden flowers, 2 cm in diameter, stand out in bold relief against the dark green forest foliage. It is worth cultivating as a garden shrub, especially in humid frost-free areas, and has proved a success in the National Botanic Garden in Salisbury. Several other members of the genus are well known subtropical garden plants; in some of these, such as *M. erythrophylla* and *M. leucophylla* from West Africa and Zaire, one of the lobes of the calyx is enlarged to about the size and shape of a leaf and is coloured bright red, yellow or white to attract insects for pollination. Although *M. arcuata* lacks this unusual device for luring insects, its flowers, massed together into compact clusters, encourage pollination.

This genus is native to Sri Lanka and the generic name is derived from a local Cingalese name. The specific name refers to the arcuate or arching branches of this species.

Africans formerly used the wood from this shrub for making bows.

134 Pentanisia schweinfurthii Hiern   *Plate 175*

common pentanisia

Family Rubiaceae

Flowers August to October.

Habitat Grassland or *Brachystegia* and other types of woodland on granite sands at altitudes of 1 000 to 1 800 m.

Distribution It is common in the open grassland of the watershed from Inyanga to Salisbury, and also along the eastern border mountains. It is found through much of tropical Africa from northern Nigeria across to the Sudan and south to Angola and Rhodesia.

General This is a perennial plant with a woody root-stock and annual herbaceous branches normally reaching 10 to 15 cm in height. It is one of the first plants to flower in spring after an early veld fire. The clusters of delicate blue flowers are very conspicuous and quite unmistakable. It is probable that it would not prove satisfactory as a garden plant because fire appears to be necessary to stimulate good flowering.

Africans use the leaves and flowers as a spinach.

There are altogether sixteen species of *Pentanisia* of which two occur in Rhodesia. The other Rhodesian species, *P. sykesii*, occurs in the Inyanga, Melsetter and Makoni districts and is distinguished from *P. schweinfurthii* by its fleshy fruit.

The generic name means 'five unequal', a reference to the fact that some of the calyx lobes are larger than others. The species is named after Professor G. A. Schweinfurth (1836-1925), a renowned German botanical explorer in Africa who first collected this species in the Sudan.

Plate 176   Plate 177

135 Scabiosa austro-africana Heine — *Plate 176*

african white scabious

Family Dipsacaceae

Flowers September to January.

Habitat Open grassland, *Brachystegia* woodland or grassy stream banks and seepage areas in drier regions.

Distribution Throughout the watershed areas of Rhodesia, but probably most common around Salisbury. It extends southwards from Kenya, Tanzania, Rwanda and Zaire to the Cape.

General For many years this species has been regarded as a form of *S. columbaria*, the european scabious which extends across to the Middle East and down into southern Africa. However, *S. columbaria* has mauve or lilac flowers and median stem leaves which are not divided, whereas the corolla of *S. austro-africana* is white or cream (though sometimes pinkish) and the median stem leaves are equally divided. There is also a difference in the length of the calyx bristles which are much longer in *S. austro-africana* than in *S. columbaria*. Apparently *S. columbaria* has not been recorded from the eastern border mountains, but it occurs in South Africa and Malawi.

Very similar to *Scabiosa* is the related genus *Cephalaria* whose species lack the conspicuous bristles on the calyx. One species, *C. pungens*, occurs in Rhodesia. .

The family takes its name from the genus *Dipsacus*, a member of which is *D. fullonum*, the fuller's teasel, which has a prickly head used for carding wool.

Members of the genus *Scabiosa* are supposed to be of use in curing scabies, and this is said to be the origin of the generic name. The specific name *austro-africana* means 'southern African' or 'South African'.

136 Momordica kirkii (Hook.f.) Jeffrey — *Plate 177*

fish-tail creeper

Family Cucurbitaceae

Flowers January to March.

Habitat Found along river banks and in thickets, occurring in association with *Adansonia*, *Colophospermum* and *Acacia*.

Distribution Zambezi and Sabi river valleys. It also occurs in Botswana, Zambia, Mozambique and Tanzania.

General This creeper climbs over bushes growing in shade under trees, forming a thick tangled mat of foliage. The stems arise each year from a large tuberous root, and die off with the approach of the dry season. The brilliant orange flowers are about 3 cm in diameter; the male flowers bear unusual fish-tail petals.

All members of the pumpkin or cucumber families have separate male and female flowers, and *M. kirkii* is no exception, although it is slightly unusual in having both types of flower on the same plant. Another peculiarity of *M. kirkii* is that the group of 1 to 4 male flowers is borne in the sinus at the base of a leaf blade — the flower peduncle is completely fused with the leaf petiole. The fruit is spindle-shaped and up to 32 mm long by 6 mm across.

The related species *M. boivinii* is rather similar in that the male flowers stick out through the basal sinus of the leaf; however, the peduncle and petiole are not fused.

There are forty-two species of *Momordica* in the Old World, most of which are African. Rhodesia has seven species, all readily separable.

The generic name *Momordica* means 'bitten', a reference to the uneven appearance of the seeds. The species was named after Sir John Kirk, who collected it on the Zambezi river in Mozambique between Sena and Lupata.

Plate 178   Plate 179

137 Lobelia decipiens Sond.   *Plate 178*

butterfly lobelia

Family Campanulaceae

Flowers September to March.

Habitat Grassland at margins of vleis, and other damp places with sparse grass cover.

Distribution Along the central watershed from the Matopo hills via Gwelo, Salisbury and Marandellas to Inyanga, Umtali and Melsetter. It occurs also at Mtoko and Fort Victoria. It is found throughout the South African highveld and down to the coast in Natal and the eastern Cape.

General This tiny perennial averages 15 to 20 cm in height and grows from a short creeping underground rhizome. There are many small species of lobelia in southern Africa, but *L. decipiens* has, for its size, perhaps the most colourful flowers. It is often found in considerable populations, all the plants having burst into flower together after a fire. Two other species which are also inclined to appear by the thousand in a favourable season are *L. filiformis* and *L. nuda*. In some areas and in some seasons the two latter species will grow in such quantities that they seem to cover the ground with a blue haze.

Lobelia is a cosmopolitan genus of between two and three hundred species. About twenty species occur in Rhodesia ranging from the giant *L. stricklandiae*, a relative of the tree-lobelias of the east African mountains, to *L. cobaltica*, a perennial species with showy dark blue flowers endemic to the Chimanimani mountains, and *L. depressa*, a prostrate vlei species.

The genus is named after Mathias de l'Obel, a Flemish botanist who was physician to James I of England. The specific name *decipiens* means 'deceptive' but what this was intended to convey is uncertain.

138 Athrixia rosmarinifolia (Schultz Bip. ex Walp.) Oliv. & Hiern

manica daisy   *Plate 179*

Family Compositae

Flowers July to September.

Habitat In *Brachystegia* and other types of woodland and in scrub and rank grass on hillsides and in valleys.

Distribution Along the eastern border mountains from Chipinga to Inyanga and eastwards along the watershed to Salisbury; also recorded from Mazoe, Concession, Umvukwes and Selukwe.

General A perennial bushy plant about 1 m tall, it makes an attractive sight in the dry grass at the end of winter. The 12 mm flower heads look somewhat like michaelmas daisies.

In South Africa, the widespread and somewhat similar species, *A. phylicoides*, known as bushman's tea, was used by Africans and Europeans as a substitute for tea, as a blood purifier and as a cough cure. *A. phylicoides* also occurs in Rhodesia in the Matopos area.

There are about twenty species in the genus, of which four, including *A. rosmarinifolia*, occur in Rhodesia. *A. foliosa* is found in the mountains of the eastern border and has wider leaves than does *A. rosmarinifolia*, and *A. fontinalis* has larger flower heads and is known only from the Chimanimani mountains and Mount Inyangani.

The generic name *Athrixia* means 'no hair' and refers to the glabrous receptacle. The foliage of the manica daisy is similar in appearance to that of the herb, rosemary — hence its specific name.

Plate 180

Plate 183

Plate 182   Plate 181

139 Bidens schimperi Schultz Bip. *Plates* 180 and 181

mnondo bur-marigold

Family Compositae

Flowers February to April.

Habitat Often in *Julbernardia globiflora* woodland, particularly along roadsides and around the bases of granite kopjes at lower altitudes. Also in mixed woodland on Kalahari Sand.

Distribution Very common in the Sabi and Odzi river basins in the Buhera and Umtali districts, but widespread elsewhere in the drier granite sandveld and on Kalahari Sand up to the Victoria Falls. It extends from Ethiopia in the north to Natal in the south.

General This species is very similar to the msasa bur-marigold, *B. steppia*. Both are annuals, 1 to 1,5 m tall, which grow in profusion in semi-shade on granite sands and have yellow flowers and finely divided leaves. However, they differ in that the barbs on the bristles of the achenes of *B. steppia* point forward, and so do not catch in clothing, whereas the bristles of *B. schimperi* are weakly barbed; the former grows at higher altitudes in wetter areas favoured by msasa trees (*Brachystegia spiciformis*), whereas *B. schimperi* is found mainly at lower drier altitudes supporting mnondo trees (*Julbernardia globiflora*).

Several familiar plants belong to the genus *Bidens*: the beautiful introduced cosmos, *B. formosa*, with its white, pink and maroon flowers which adorn roadsides in Mashonaland and elsewhere; the yellow cosmos, *B. sulphurea*, another naturalised species; and the white- and yellow-flowered blackjacks, *B. pilosa* and *B. biternata*, both weeds of cultivation.

Bidens means 'two-toothed', a reference to the bristles on the achene. W. G. Schimper was a German botanist who collected in Ethiopia in the middle of the last century.

140 Berkheya zeyheri (Sond. & Harv.) Oliv. & Hiern

woodland sun daisy *Plates* 182 and 183

Family Compositae

Flowers November to February.

Habitat Principally in open *Brachystegia spiciformis*, *B. boehmii* and *Julbernardia* woodland. Also in montane grassland over granite and dolerite up to altitudes of 2 100 m.

Distribution Along all the watershed areas in the eastern part of Rhodesia, extending west to Salisbury through much of Mashonaland, and south to Zimbabwe. Occurs also in Tanzania, Zambia, Malawi and Mozambique, and south to the Transvaal, Swaziland and Natal.

General The woodland sun daisy has annual erect stems arising from a perennial root-stock and stands 50 to 60 cm tall. The flower head is about 5 cm in diameter and is easily recognisable because of the numerous fine bristly bracts which enclose the composite head. As is normal in the daisy family, the 'flower' is actually a tightly packed cluster of individual flowers. The outer ones, known as ray florets, simulate petals by having a petaloid limb on one side of the tubular flower, whereas the central flowers, comprising the disc, are unadorned and are known as tubular florets.

There are about ninety species of *Berkheya* recognised, all of which are African. Four species occur in Rhodesia: *B. echinacea* subsp. *polyacantha* occurs at Inyanga; *B. setifera*, a South African species which has a very prickly and thistle-like stem, extends as far north as Melsetter and Himalaya in Rhodesia; and *B. radula*, another South African species, occurs from the Matopo hills to Rusape but does not reach the eastern districts.

The genus is named after M. J. L. de Berkhey, a Dutch botanist. Carl Zeyher (1799-1868) was a German plant collector who lived most of his life in South Africa.

Plate 184

Plate 185

141 Gazania krebsiana Less.   *Plate 184*

subsp. **serrulata** (DC.) Roessler

grassland gazania

Family   Compositae

Flowers   August to October.

Habitat   Open grassland and vlei margins at altitudes ranging between 1 350 and 1 800 m.

Distribution   Mainly on high ground in Manicaland from Chipinga to Inyanga, but also along the watershed to Salisbury and southward towards Bulawayo. This subspecies extends via Zambia, Malawi and Mozambique into Tanzania, and is very common on the highveld of the Transvaal and Orange Free State. In the eastern Cape it is replaced by the typical subspecies.

General   This flower, stimulated by veld burning, is one of the first harbingers of spring. The plant is a perennial, only a few centimetres tall, with yellow flower heads about 4 cm in diameter; the populations of this subspecies in South Africa have either white or yellow heads. The magnificent variety, var. *arctotoides*, occurs in South Africa in Namaqualand and the Karoo; its deep orange flowers have an eye-spot at the base of each 'petal'. This spot, usually bronzy-green, is found occasionally in the white and yellow forms.

There are forty species of *Gazania*, all of which occur in South Africa; only the one is found in Rhodesia.

The generic name is probably derived from the Greek for wealth, an allusion to the golden flowers of many of the species. George L. E. Krebs (1792-1844) was a German who farmed near Bedford in the eastern Cape and collected plants and birds.

142 Erythrocephalum zambesianum Hiern   *Plate 185*

red rays

Family   Compositae

Flowers   December to March.

Habitat   *Brachystegia* woodland in semi-shade, usually on stony hillsides, in higher rainfall areas.

Distribution   Principally along the eastern border from Chipinga to Inyanga, but also along the watershed at least as far as Rusape. It is found in the adjacent parts of Mozambique, as well as Zambia, Malawi and Tanzania.

General   This plant is a perennial herb up to 60 cm tall, branching at the base. The silvery grey leaves with their white velvety undersides form a striking contrast to the rich crimson flower heads, which are up to 5 cm in diameter. This species is sufficiently attractive to warrant a place in the garden, and fully merits the attention of plant breeders in order to develop plants with larger and more uniform heads.

This is the only showy member of the genus in Rhodesia. Three further species occur in Zambia and two others are found in Mozambique.

The generic name means 'red head'. Contrary to the implications of the specific name, this species does not occur in the Zambezi valley; one of the types was collected by Sir John Kirk in the Manganja Hills near the Shire river on his expedition up the Zambezi with David Livingstone.

Plate 186   Plate 187

143 Gerbera viridifolia (DC.) Schultz Bip. *Plate* 186

blushing barberton daisy

Family   Compositae

Flowers   October to December.

Habitat   Open · grassland or *Brachystegia spiciformis* (msasa), *B. boehmii* (mfuti) and other types of woodland.

Distribution   Common in Mashonaland around Salisbury, but extends to the eastern border mountains, along the central watershed to Zimbabwe and the Lundi escarpment, and north to the Urungwe Tribal Trust Land. It occurs from Zaire, Sudan, Ethiopia and Somalia southwards to the Cape Province.

General   This perennial herb has leaves arising from ground level and flower stems up to 30 cm tall. Both the unopened and the faded heads tend to hang demurely, showing the deep pink flush on the under sides of the ray florets. The leaves are green on both the upper and under surfaces, a feature which has led to the specific name *viridifolia*. The green leaves and white flowers serve to distinguish it from *G. ambigua* which occurs in vleis on the highveld of Rhodesia and has yellow flowers. The genus is named after Franz Gerber, a German naturalist.

The scarlet *G. jamesonii* is the original barberton daisy which occurs wild in the eastern Transvaal. Many cultivars based on this species have been developed and, by interbreeding with other species, an attractive array of colours, flower sizes and petal widths has been produced.

144 Haplocarpha scaposa Harv. *Plate* 187

common haplocarpha

Family   Compositae

Flowers   November to January.

Habitat   Montane grassland, vlei margins, sparse short grass or on patches of bare soil overlying granite or dolerite.

Distribution   Mainly in the mountains of the eastern border but also along the watershed wherever damp grassland is found. This species is widespread in the grasslands of South Africa, and occurs also in Zambia and Malawi.

General   This perennial herb has a rosette of very broad leathery leaves which sometimes lie almost flat on the ground. The leaves, 15 cm in length, have a thick woolly coat below and prominent raised veins. The 3 cm wide flower heads are borne on stems 20 to 30 cm tall; a leafless flower stem of this type is known as a scape — hence the specific name. The generic name means 'single scale' and refers to the ring of hairs or pappus of the achene or seed. This species bears some resemblance to the yellow-flowered *Gerbera ambigua* which grows in similar sites, but the broader leaves with their prominent, almost parallel, veins on the underside distinguish it from the latter.

There are ten African species of *Haplocarpha* of which only two occur in Rhodesia. The other species, *H. nervosa*, is known in Rhodesia only from the summit of Inyangani. It extends southwards to Lesotho and the Cape.

Plate 188

Plate 189

145 Helichrysum adenocarpum DC.   *Plate 188*

fairy everlasting

Family   Compositae

Flowers   Mainly from February to May.

Habitat   Short open montane grassland, often at edges of marshy ground.

Distribution   In Rhodesia, almost confined to the eastern border mountains from Inyangani south to the Chimanimani range and Mount Selinda. However, it also occurs sparingly along the watershed as far as Rusape and Marandellas, and on Gorongosa mountain in Mozambique. Its range extends southwards via the Soutpansberg and the mountains of the eastern Transvaal and Swaziland as far as the eastern Cape.

General   This attractive plant is a perennial 20 to 50 cm tall. The branching stems grow from a basal rosette of grey woolly leaves. The involucral bracts which give the colour to the flower head vary from crimson to pink, pink and white, or very rarely just white. The small yellow tubular florets are tightly packed in the centre of the composite flower head.

There are some three hundred African species of *Helichrysum* of which over forty occur in Rhodesia.

The generic name *Helichrysum*, meaning 'golden sun', is very apt since many species are a rich golden yellow in colour. The specific name *adenocarpum* means 'glandular fruit' and refers to the glandular achenes.

Other Rhodesian species that have at least some reddish colour in their involucral bracts are the Chimanimani endemic *H. rhodellum*, the woodland plant *H. rhodolepis*, the small prostrate weed *H. argyrosphaerum*, and the widespread *H. leptolepis*.

146 Helichrysum nitens DC.   *Plate 189*

shining everlasting

Family   Compositae

Flowers   March to October.

Habitat   Montane grassland and stony hillsides at altitudes ranging between 1 500 and 2 000 m.

Distribution   Extremely common on the mountains in Manicaland from Mount Inyangani to the Chimanimanis; it is very conspicuous on the Vumba mountains in grassland or on road cuttings. Occasionally found elsewhere in Rhodesia in wet high areas such as Mount Buhwa in the Belingwe District and near Rusape. It occurs also in Mozambique and Angola and north through Zambia and Malawi to Zaire and Tanzania.

General   This is a particularly striking species with its bright yellow flower heads, 2 to 3 cm in diameter, contrasting with the soft silvery grey velvety leaves. The plants are usually 50 to 60 cm tall, but they may reach 1 m or more.

The specific name *nitens* is derived from Latin and means 'polished' or 'shining', a term which aptly describes the golden involucral bracts.

Both *H. adenocarpum* and *H. nitens* are among the everlastings that are popular for dried flower arrangements. Suitable specimens can be prepared by being hung upside-down in a dark cupboard until dry, or buried for a week or two in a mixture of fine sand and gypsum.

In former times Africans extracted a crude salt by burning the plants and dissolving the ash.

Other common yellow-flowered species in Rhodesia are *H. splendidum* and *H. odoratissimum* which are very abundant on montane grassland at Inyanga. *H. kraussii* is a widespread woodland species which is particularly common in over-grazed areas or on poor soils.

Plate 190

Plate 191

147 Hypericophyllum compositarum Steetz   *Plate* 190

orange tassels

Family   Compositae

Flowers   March to June.

Habitat   *Brachystegia boehmii* and *B. spiciformis* woodland, frequently on granite kopjes, at altitudes ranging between 1 000 and 1 500 m.

Distribution   From Fort Victoria, Chibi, Belingwe and Bikita in the south through much of Mashonaland and Manicaland to Zambia, Malawi and Mozambique, and as far north as Tanzania.

General   This is a perennial herb with annual stems reaching 1,5 m in height. The flower heads are about 2 cm in diameter. There are no ray florets; the bright orange tubular disc florets attract the insect pollinators.

The generic name *Hypericophyllum* means 'with leaves like a hypericum'. The specific name means 'belonging to the Compositae'.

There are about seven species of *Hypericophyllum*, all of which are confined to tropical Africa. The only other species to occur in Rhodesia is *H. elatum*, a more robust plant with larger flower heads, which occurs in the Chipinga area in Rhodesia, the Soutpansberg in South Africa, and also in Mozambique, Malawi, Zambia and Tanzania.

148 Helichrysum herbaceum (Andr.) Sweet   *Plate* 191

monkey-tail everlasting

Family   Compositae

Synonym   *H. squamosum*

Flowers   February to May.

Habitat   Open montane grassland on leached acidic sandy soils overlying granite, at altitudes of 1 800 m or more.

Distribution   Inyanga mountains and the Rhodes Inyanga National Park, thence along the eastern border to the Chimanimani mountains and high areas around Melsetter. It occurs also on the Nyika plateau in northern Malawi and Zambia, and in southern Tanzania. In South Africa it is found along the Drakensberg and as far south as Humansdorp in the southern Cape.

General   This perennial plant grows from creeping underground rhizomes. Its 25 cm tall flowering stems look like grey monkey tails. The straw yellow flower heads glisten in the sun amongst the browning grass of autumn and, because of their numbers, are a conspicuous and attractive sight.

The specific name *herbaceum* means 'yellow-green' and refers to the yellowish green involucral bracts.

Plate 192

Plate 193

149 Senecio sceleratus Schweickerdt *Plate* 192

noxious ragwort

Family Compositae

Flowers September to February.

Habitat Montane grassland and vlei margins, often on heavily over-grazed or fire-swept hillsides.

Distribution On eastern border mountains and along the central watershed to Marandellas and Salisbury. It occurs also at Fort Victoria and Bikita. It extends northwards to Zambia and Malawi and south to the Transvaal.

General *S. sceleratus* belongs to a group of closely related species which includes *S. latifolius*, *S. retrorsus*, *S. venosus* and *S. pergamentaceus*. These are all erect plants which have annual flowering stems arising from a perennial root-stock and broadish leaves that clasp the stem. The distinctions between these species are not always clear and it seems likely that some changes will be made when this group is revised. However, *S. sceleratus* may be distinguished from *S. latifolius* in having leaves which are opaque, whereas the latter has leaves with reticulate veining that can be seen readily if the leaf is held up to the light.

The young shoots of *S. sceleratus* may appear in August before the grass greens up, at which time they are most likely to be grazed by livestock. This species contains a cumulative poison which is highly toxic to cattle and horses and for which there is no effective antidote — hence the specific name *sceleratus* meaning noxious. Death may occur one to three months after the plant has been ingested. Prevention of *Senecio* poisoning lies mainly in good veld management and supplementary feeding of livestock at critical times. About fifty other species of *Senecio* occur in Rhodesia, but so far only *S. sceleratus* has proved to be toxic.

150 Senecio tamoides DC. *Plate* 193

canary creeper

Family Compositae

Flowers April to July.

Habitat Forest margins and river banks in high rainfall areas.

Distribution Along the eastern border mountains from the Pungwe river to the Rusitu river. It occurs in Mozambique and possibly also in Malawi. In South Africa it is found in forests on the mountains of the eastern Transvaal and southwards to the eastern Cape.

General This species climbs in amongst, or over, bushes up to 3 m tall. The trusses of flowers are 12 to 15 cm in diameter with the individual composite flower heads measuring about 15 mm across. The vivid splash of yellow that this creeper provides in autumn has made it a favourite with gardeners and it is now widely cultivated. It is particularly effective when grown on a trellis against a wall or up an evergreen tree. Propagation is easiest from mature stem cuttings or root division; a warm, well watered fertile soil with adequate compost is preferred. It is evergreen in frost-free areas, but dies back under colder conditions.

The name *Senecio* was used by Pliny and is derived from *senex* which means 'old man'. This is an allusion to the white hairs of the pappus.

The specific name *tamoides* means 'like *Tamus communis*'. The latter is a climber found in Europe; although its leaves somewhat resemble those of *S. tamoides*, the two are quite unrelated.

Glossary

Achene   a small-seeded indehiscent fruit

Acuminate   terminating in a small sharp point

Appressed   pressed close to the plant, usually applied to hairs

Annual   a plant that completes its life cycle in twelve months and then dies

Anther   the part of the stamen which bears the pollen

Brachystegia   a genus of leguminous trees which are dominant or co-dominant over much of the higher ground in Rhodesia

Bract   a modified leaf subtending a flower or part of an inflorescence

Bulb   a fleshy underground portion of a plant consisting of swollen leaf-bases, as in an onion

Bulbils   bulbs arising around a mother bulb

Calyx   the outermost whorl of a flower (usually green) consisting of free or joined sepals which help to protect the petals whilst the flower is still in bud

Capsule   a dry dehiscent fruit composed of more than one carpel

Carpel   one of the divisions of the ovary or fruit

Concolorous   of a uniform colour

Connective   the tissue or part of the filament connecting the two cells of an anther

Corm   a short tuberous root-stock, often outwardly resembling a bulb but not layered within

Corolla   the inner whorl of a flower consisting of free or joined petals

Cultivar   a form produced and persisting under cultivation, and maintained as an entity under artificial conditions by horticulture

Cyme   a repeatedly branched inflorescence in which the central flowers open first

Deciduous   falling off, usually in winter

Dehiscent   opening spontaneously along definite lines or sutures

Disc florets   the tubular central florets as opposed to the ray florets in Compositae flower heads

Diuretic   causing excessive discharge of urine

Endemic   confined to a particular area and not found elsewhere

Epicalyx   a series of bracts below a flower which resemble an extra calyx

Epiphyte   a plant which habitually grows upon another plant but, unlike a parasite, does not derive any of its food from it

Ericoid   with very reduced leaves like those of a heath

Exserted   projecting beyond, e.g. stamens from a corolla tube

Filament   the stalk of a stamen which bears the anthers

Glabrous   smooth and hairless

Gland   a secreting organ sunk in or protruding from the surface of a plant

Glaucous   blue-grey or covered with a blue-grey bloom

Habit   life-form, for example bush, tree or climber

Habitat   the environment in which a plant grows

Hastate   refers to a leaf with pointed or triangular lobes at the base

Herb   any plant which is not woody

Herbaceous   not woody

Indehiscent   not opening spontaneously along definite lines or sutures

Inferior   when describing an ovary it refers to the fact that it is situated below the other parts of the flower

Inflorescence   the aggregation and arrangement of the flowers on a plant

Involucral   forming an involucre, as involucral bracts

Involucre   a number of bracts surrounding or just below a flower or flower head

Keel   lower petal in Leguminosae flowers, often shaped like the keel of a boat

Leaflet   unit or part of a compound leaf

Liane   a large woody climber, often with rope-like stems

Linear   long and narrow with parallel sides

Lip   one of the portions of a corolla that is divided unequally into two, or the lower petal of an orchid

Obovate   shaped like an inverted egg, widest above the middle

Ovary   the part of the flower that encloses the immature seeds

Pan   a depression with no outlet which fills with water, usually for only part of the year

Papillae   small nipple-like prominences

Pappus   the modified calyx in the Compositae that usually takes the form of a ring of hairs or scales and often persists on the end of the fruit

Parasite   a plant which derives its nourishment from another plant to which it is attached

Pedicel   an individual flower stalk

Peduncle   the stalk of an inflorescence or part of an inflorescence

Perennial   living for three or more years

Perianth   the sepals and petals of a flower

Persistent   not falling off

Petal   one of the inner whorl of perianth segments, often brightly coloured

Petiole   leaf stalk

Prostrate   lying flat on the ground

Pubescence   covering of hairs

Pubescent   shortly and softly hairy

Raceme   an unbranched often spike-like inflorescence in which the individual flowers are stalked

Rachis   axis or midrib of a compound leaf

Ray florets   the marginal strap-shaped florets in a composite flower as opposed to the central disc florets

Revolute   rolled

Rhizome   underground stem, usually growing parallel to the soil surface

Samara   an indehiscent dry fruit or seed provided with a wing

Sepal   a segment of the calyx or outer whorl of the perianth

Sinus   recess between the teeth or lobes of a leaf margin

Spadix   a dense flower spike which has a fleshy axis, as found in the Araceae

Spathe   a large sheath-like bract

Spur   a hollow, usually conical, outgrowth of the perianth

Stamen   the pollen-bearing part of a flowering plant, typically consisting of an anther borne on a filament

Staminode   an infertile, usually somewhat modified, stamen

Standard   the upper petal in Leguminosae flowers

Stellate   star-shaped

Stigma   the part of the flower which receives the pollen, usually situated on the end of the style

Style   the elongated tip of the ovary which bears the stigma

Subtending   embracing or supporting at the base

Superior   when describing an ovary, it refers to the fact that it is inserted above the perianth segments

Tendril   a modified stem or leaf forming a climbing organ

Terrestrial   growing on the ground

Truncate   cut off abruptly at the end, not rounded or pointed

Tuber   a swollen underground portion of a stem or root

Umbel   an inflorescence in which the peduncles or pedicels radiate from a single point

Viscid   sticky

Vlei   a loose term applied to both seasonally marshy ground and ground that is permanently wet

Index of scientific names

Species	No.	Location		
Dolichos kilimandscharicus	3481	Inyanga	72	49
Elephantorrhiza elephantina	2812	Great Dyke, Banket	78	53
Erica swynnertonii	2319	Inyanga	120	88
Eriosema engleranum	2120	Marandellas	80	55
Eriosema psoraleoides	4434	Inyazura	81	56
Erythrocephalum zambesianum	2292	Umtali	185	142
Eucomis autumnalis	2872	Watsomba, Umtali	16	4
Eulophia cucullata	2727	Vumba, Umtali	53	33
Eulophia zeyheri	2731	Chipinga	54	34
Gazania krebsiana	2461	Melsetter	184	141
Gerbera viridifolia	4426	Salisbury	186	143
Gladiolus gazensis	2459	Melsetter	37	19
Gladiolus melleri	4419	Salisbury	38	20
Gladiolus natalensis	3461	Inyanga	39	21
Gladiolus natalensis	—	Norton	40	21
Gloriosa superba	4476	Selborne, Inyanga	13	3
Gloriosa superba	2550	Salisbury	14	3
Gloriosa superba	—	Victoria Falls	15	3
Glossostelma carsonii	2531	Umtali	128	94
Gnidia kraussiana	4421	Salisbury	108	81
Gnidia kraussiana	—	Great Dyke, Umvukwes	109	81
Gossypium herbaceum	3423	Birchenough bridge	96	69
Graderia scabra	2127	Stapleford, Umtali	149	111
Haemanthus multiflorus	1291	Matopo hills, Bulawayo	30	13
Haemanthus multiflorus	—	Victoria Falls	31	13
Haemanthus pole-evansii	2873	Pungwe falls, Inyanga	32	14
Haplocarpha scaposa	4431	Inyanga	187	144
Harpagophytum procumbens	4468	Antelope Mine, Matopos	163	122
Helichrysum adenocarpum	2172	Chimanimani mountains	188	145
Helichrysum herbaceum	4409	Inyanga	191	148
Helichrysum nitens	2266	Mount Inyangani	189	146
Hibiscus aethiopicus	2824	Inyanga	97	70
Hibiscus burtt-davyi	2854	Chimanimani mountains	99	72
Hibiscus caesius	2767	Chipinga	98	71
Hibiscus dongolensis	3182	Rupisi, Sabi valley	101	74
Hibiscus meeusei	2764	Melsetter	100	73
Hibiscus rhodanthus	2272	Great Dyke, Umvukwes	103	76
Holothrix randii	2716	Headlands	50	30
Hypericophyllum compositarum	2688	Zimbabwe, Fort Victoria	190	147
Hypericum revolutum	2822	Inyanga	107	80
Hypericum roeperanum	1224	Melsetter	106	79
Hypoxis obtusa	2714	Headlands	33	15
Indigofera dimidiata	2431	Mount Inyangani	82	57
Indigofera hilaris	2117	Marandellas	83	58
Ipomoea kituiensis	2446	Lower Buhera	130,131	96
Ipomoea ommaneyi	3490	Insiza, Bulawayo	132	97
Ipomoea shirambensis	2791	Devuli, Sabi valley	133	98
Justicia elegantula	2125	Marandellas	169	128
Kaempferia aethiopica	2282	Burma valley, Umtali	46	27
Kaempferia decora	2529	Umtali	45	26
Kaempferia rosea	3485	Wankie	47,48	28
Kniphofia linearifolia	2847	Chimanimani mountains	17	5
Kniphofia linearifolia	2306	Erin, Inyanga	18	5
Lantana trifolia	2303	Umtali	138	101
Lapeirousia odoratissima	2548	Salisbury	42	23
Leonotis dysophylla	3454	Bulawayo	141	103
Leptactina benguelensis	2715	Headlands	173	132
Leucospermum saxosum	2245	Chimanimani mountains	61	40

Species	No.	Locality		
Lobelia decipiens	2766	Melsetter	178	137
Loranthus braunii	4477	Bromley	62	41
Loranthus curviflorus	2770	Fort Victoria	63	42
Melhania acuminata	2302	Hot Springs, Sabi valley	104	77
Merremia kentrocaulos	4439	Hot Springs, Sabi valley	134	99
Momordica kirkii	2760	Hot Springs, Sabi valley	177	136
Monsonia biflora	4423	Salisbury	88	63
Moraea spathulata	3477	Melsetter	43	24
Mucuna coriacea	2697	Ngorima, Melsetter	84	59
Mundulea sericea	3474	Rusape	85	60
Mussaenda arcuata	2684	Vumba, Umtali	174	133
Nymphaea petersiana	2691	Mutema, Sabi valley	65	44
Nymphaea petersiana	—	Chibuwe, Sabi valley	66	44
Oenostachys zambesiacus	1668	Nyamandhlovu	44	25
Oxalis semiloba	4403	Inyanga Downs	92	66
Pavonia urens	2313	Erin, Inyanga	102	75
Pelargonium luridum	4429	Umtali	89	64
Pentanisia schweinfurthii	2713	Headlands	175	134
Podranea brycei	4478	Ngorima, Melsetter	156,157	117
Polygala virgata	2113	Umtali	94,95	68
Protea angolensis	2023	Rusape	57	37
Protea angolensis	2024	Rusape	58	37
Protea gazensis	4437	Melsetter	59	38
Protea welwitschii	2022	Chimanimani mountains	60	39
Pseudarthria hookeri	2076	Umtali	86	61
Pycnostachys stuhlmannii	3202	The Range, Enkeldoorn	144	106
Pycnostachys urticifolia	4479	Marandellas	143	105
Rhamphicarpa tubulosa	2676	Salisbury	150	112
Rhigozum zambesiacum	2829	Nyanyadzi, Sabi valley	158,159	118
Ruspolia hypocrateriformis	2874	Chipinga district	172	131
Satyrium longicauda	2427	Mount Inyangani	55	35
Satyrium neglectum	2148	Mount Inyangani	56	36
Scabiosa austro-africana	4424	Salisbury	176	135
Scutellaria paucifolia	2814	Inyanga	142	104
Selago thyrsoidea	2185	Inyanga Downs	154,155	116
Senecio sceleratus	3476	Mutema, Chipinga	192	149
Senecio tamoides	2698	Vumba, Umtali	193	150
Sesamum alatum	2739	Sabi river, Chipinga	161	120
Solanum panduriforme	2537	Umtali	146	108
Sopubia mannii	2434	Mount Inyangani	151	113
Sphedamnocarpus pruriens	2334	Melsetter	93	67
Streptocarpus eylesii	2294	Umtali	165	124
Streptocarpus michelmorei	2496	Ngorima, Melsetter	164	123
Striga elegans	2295	Mtarazi falls, Inyanga	153	115
Strophanthus kombe	2813	Hot Springs, Sabi valley	126	92
Sutera carvalhoi	2463	Inyanga	152	114
Talinum arnotii	2541	Rupisi, Sabi valley	64	43
Thunbergia alata	2765	Melsetter	170	129
Thunbergia lancifolia	4480	Salisbury	171	130
Tribulus zeyheri	3155	Beitbridge	90,91	65
Trichodesma physaloides	3430	Salisbury	139,140	102
Turbina holubii	2237	Moosgwe, Melsetter	135,137	100
Turbina holubii	2689	Insiza, Bulawayo	136	100
Tylosema fassoglensis	3483	Victoria Falls	79	54
Vigna frutescens	2270	Great Dyke, Umvukwes	87	62
Wormskioldia longepedunculata	4481	Umtali	105	78
Xerophyta villosa	2670	Maranke, Umtali	34	16
Zantedeschia albomaculata	2675	Salisbury	11	1

Index of common names

Wild Flowers of Rhodesia

This book provides a ready and convenient means of identifying some of the showy indigenous wild flowers of Rhodesia. Most of the species selected are commonly found, although a few of the more attractive rare plants have been included.

The descriptions of the species, each accompanied by beautiful full-colour plates, include notes on appearance, habitat, flowering times, distribution, similar and related species, and commercial and medicinal uses.

Darrel Plowes, a well known photographer and distinguished natural historian, is Provincial Agricultural Officer for Manicaland.

Robert Drummond, Keeper of the National Herbarium, Salisbury, is co-author of Common Trees of the Highveld, also published by Longman.

Also available from Longman

Flowers of the Veld, by Kay Linley and Bryan Baker

Aloes of Rhodesia, by Oliver West

Common Trees of the Highveld, by Robert Drummond and Keith Coates Palgrave

Longman